JAMESTOWN EDUCATION

# *Reading Science*

## Strategies for English Language Learners

**High Beginning**

McGraw Hill Glencoe

New York, New York    Columbus, Ohio    Chicago, Illinois    Peoria, Illinois    Woodland Hills, California

JAMESTOWN EDUCATION

**Image Credits: Cover** (prism)ThinkStock, (satellite)CORBIS, (globe)Creatas, (others)Getty Images.

Glencoe

The *McGraw·Hill* Companies

Send all inquiries to:
Glencoe/McGraw-Hill
8787 Orion Place
Columbus, OH 43240-4027

ISBN 0-07-872914-9 (Student Edition)
ISBN 0-07-872917-3 (Teacher Edition)

Printed in the United States of America.

1 2 3 4 5 6 7 8 9 10  066  11 10 09 08 07 06

# Contents

Reading is one of the fastest ways for you to get information. *Reading Science* can help you improve the way you read and understand science topics. You will also learn how to improve your test-taking skills.

## Before You Read

These steps can help you *preview* an article and get an idea of what it is about.

**Read the title.** Ask yourself "What can I learn from the title?" and "What do I already know about this subject?"

**Read the first sentence or two.** The writer wants to catch your attention in the first sentence or two. You may also find out what you are about to learn.

**Skim the entire article.** Look over the article quickly for words that may help you understand it. Jot down unfamiliar words in your Personal Dictionary. You can ask someone later what they mean.

**Participate in class discussions.** Your teacher may show you pictures or objects and ask you questions about them. Try to answer the questions.

## While You Read

Here are some tips to help you make sense of what you read:

**Concentrate.** If your mind wanders, remind yourself of what you learned when you previewed the article.

**Ask yourself questions.** Ask yourself "What does this mean?" or "How can I use this information?"

**Look for the topic of each paragraph.** Each paragraph has a main idea. The other sentences build on that idea. Find all of the main ideas to understand the entire article.

**Refer to the vocabulary you have learned.** The words in dark type will remind you of what you learned in the Vocabulary section. For more help, refer to the previous page.

## After You Read

The activities in *Reading Science* will help you practice different ways to learn.

**A. Organizing Ideas** Webs, charts, and tables will help you organize information from the article. Sometimes you will create your own art.

**B. Comprehension Skills** will help you recall facts and understand ideas.

**C. Reading Strategies** will suggest ways to make sense of what you read.

**D. Expanding Vocabulary** will teach you more about the vocabulary you learned before and during reading.

## Vocabulary Assessment

After every five lessons, you can try out what you have learned. Activities, such as postcards and advertisements, show you how the vocabulary can be useful and fun in everyday life. Enjoy!

# Pronunciation Key

| | | | |
|---|---|---|---|
| **a** | as in *an* or *cat* | **k** | as in *kitchen, book, mock,* or *cool* |
| **ä** | as in *father* or *arm* | **l** | as in *look, alive, heel, tall,* or *follow* |
| **ā** | as in *made, say,* or *maid* | **m** | as in *me, imagine,* or *seem* |
| **e** | as in *wet* or *sell* | **n** | as in *no, inside, inning,* or *fun* |
| **ē** | as in *he, see, mean, niece,* or *lovely* | **ng** | as in *singer, bring,* or *drink* |
| **i** | as in *in* or *fit* | **p** | as in *put, open,* or *drop* |
| **ī** | as in *I, mine, sigh, die,* or *my* | **r** | as in *run, form,* or *wear* |
| **o** | as in *on* or *not* | **s** | as in *socks, herself,* or *miss* |
| **ō** | as in *fold, boat, own,* or *foe* | **sh** | as in *should, washing,* or *hash* |
| **ô** | as in *or, oar, naughty, awe,* or *ball* | **t** | as in *too, enter, mitten,* or *sit* |
| **oo** | as in *good, would,* or *put* | **th** | as in *think, nothing,* or *tooth* |
| **ōō** | as in *roof* or *blue* | **th** | as in *there, either,* or *smooth* |
| **oi** | as in *noise* or *joy* | **v** | as in *vote, even,* or *love* |
| **ou** | as in *loud* or *now* | **w** | as in *well* or *away* |
| **u** | as in *must* or *cover* | **y** | as in *yellow* or *canyon* |
| **ū** | as in *pure, cue, few,* or *feud* | **z** | as in *zoo, hazy,* or *sizes* |
| **ur** | as in *turn, fern, heard, bird,* or *word* | **zh** | as in *seizure, measure,* or *mirage* |
| **ə** | as in *awhile, model, second,* or *column* | **N** | as in *bonjour* (vowel before the **N** is nasal) |
| **f** | as in *fat, before, beef, stuff, graph,* or *rough* | **KH** | as in *loch* (or German *ach*) |
| **g** | as in *give, again,* or *dog* | | |
| **h** | as in *hat, whole,* or *ahead* | | |

# Using Energy to Ride a Bike

## Before You Read

**Tip!** **Think about what you know.** Read the lesson title above. Think about what you already know about riding a bike. Is it hard to ride a bike?

## Vocabulary

The content-area and academic English words below appear in "Using Energy to Ride a Bike." Read the definitions and the example sentences.

### Content-Area Words

**fuel** (fū′əl) material such as coal, wood, or oil that can be burned to produce power
  *Example:* Gasoline can be used as *fuel* for a car.

**energy** (en′ər jē) power applied forcefully in order to do work
  *Example:* The *energy* for a lamp comes from electricity.

**transfer** (trans′ fur) to move from one person, place, or thing to another
  *Example:* Buses *transfer* students from home to school.

**gravity** (grav′ə tē) the pull or force that Earth puts on things at or near its surface
  *Example:* When you throw something in the air, *gravity* makes it come down.

**cables** (kā′bəlz) strong, thick, heavy steel or fiber ropes
  *Example:* Elevators have *cables* that attach them to ceilings and move them up and down.

### Academic English

**create** (krē āt′) to cause to be
  *Example:* An experienced cook can *create* a delicious meal quickly.

**layer** (lā′ər) one thickness laid over or under another
  *Example:* A coat provides a warm *layer* over other clothes.

Answer the questions below. Circle the part of each question that is the answer. The first one has been done for you.

1. Would you use *cables* to (attach things) or cut them apart?
2. Would an airplane or a kite need *fuel?*
3. Would it take more *energy* to run a race or watch a movie?
4. When you jump, does *gravity* make you go higher or bring you back to the ground?
5. Does a band *create* music or paintings?
6. To *transfer* books from one shelf to another, would you move them or replace them?
7. Which has a *layer* of fur on its body, a dog or a bird?

**Dictionary** Now skim the article and look for other words that are new to you. Write each new word and its definition in the Personal Dictionary.

# While You Read

**Tip!** **Think about why you read.** Do you own a bike? Do you know how bikes work? Write a question about bikes that you would like to know the answer to. As you read, you may find the answer.

# Using Energy to Ride a Bike

1 How do the cereal, milk, and orange juice you had for breakfast help you ride your bike? The food that you eat is **fuel** for your body. Your body turns this fuel into **energy.** Your body is always making and using energy.

You know that your body can **transfer** energy from your stomach to your
5 muscles. In the same way, a bike is able to transfer energy from its pedals to its wheels. The pedals are attached to a cogwheel, a wheel with metal points that stick out from its outside edge. A chain connects this cogwheel with a smaller one that is attached to the rear wheel. As the larger cogwheel turns, the chain pulls the rear cogwheel to turn the rear wheel. As the rear wheel begins to turn, the front
10 wheel begins to turn too.

Once you get the bike started, the wheels allow it to roll easily. When one surface rolls over another, the movement causes friction, or scraping, between surfaces. Friction slows you down. Bike tires are narrow. There is little friction when the small surface of a bike tire rolls across the ground. Bike wheels are
15 lightweight. It takes less energy to turn a light wheel than it does to turn a heavy one. However, lightweight wheels still have to be strong enough to hold the weight of the bike and the rider. This is the reason that wheels have spokes—to add strength.

Why do you have to pedal harder when going up a hill than you do going
20 down? You need more energy to overcome the force of **gravity.** You must use more force against the pull of gravity as you go uphill.

When you want to stop your bike, you squeeze the hand brakes. These brakes pull **cables** that in turn pull pads against the rim of the wheel. The pads **create** friction on the rim and slow the wheel down until the bike stops.

25 Remember to wear a helmet when you ride your bike. If you fell off your bike, you could hit your head. This could cause serious harm to your brain. Most helmets have a hard shell with a **layer** of stiff foam under it. If your head hits the pavement, the foam can take up most of the energy of the bump. Be sure that your helmet has a strong strap to keep it on your head. When you fall off a bike, you
30 can hit your head more than once.

So eat your breakfast, buckle on your helmet, and have a good ride!

**LANGUAGE CONNECTION**

The word *pedals* is used here as a noun. *Pedal* is also a verb that explains how to move your feet to turn bike wheels. Can you find *pedal* used as a verb in this article?

**CONTENT CONNECTION**

Think of some other activities in which helmets are used. What do these activities have in common?

# After You Read

## A. Organizing Ideas

**How do you make a bike start and stop moving?** Complete the organizer below. Write down the steps needed to start and stop a bike. Find the information in the article. You may add boxes of your own to add more details. The first box has been done for you.

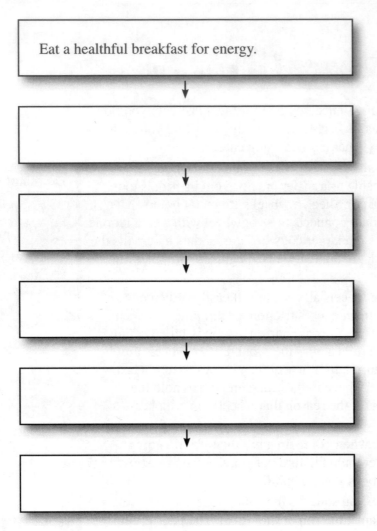

Eat a healthful breakfast for energy.

What did you learn by completing this organizer? Write two or more sentences about what you learned that you did not know before. Did the organizer help you understand the article? How?

_____

_____

_____

_____

## B. Comprehension Skills

**Tip!** **Think about how to find answers.** Look back at what you read. The information is in the text, but you may have to look in several sentences to find it.

Mark box **a, b,** or **c** with an **X** before the choice that best completes each sentence.

### Recalling Facts

1. Food is fuel that the body turns into
   - ☐ **a.** muscle.
   - ☐ **b.** action.
   - ☐ **c.** energy.

2. The pedals of a bike are attached to
   - ☐ **a.** a cogwheel.
   - ☐ **b.** the back wheel.
   - ☐ **c.** the spokes.

3. You have to pedal harder to go uphill because
   - ☐ **a.** you have to overcome the force of gravity.
   - ☐ **b.** bike tires are narrow.
   - ☐ **c.** riding up a hill creates more energy.

4. Brakes slow down a bike by using
   - ☐ **a.** the rear cogwheel.
   - ☐ **b.** gravity.
   - ☐ **c.** friction.

5. A helmet helps protect the head in a fall by
   - ☐ **a.** using the force of gravity.
   - ☐ **b.** taking up energy.
   - ☐ **c.** slowing down.

### Understanding Ideas

1. From the article, you can conclude that
   - ☐ **a.** the body can change food into the energy needed for riding a bike.
   - ☐ **b.** riding a bike creates energy.
   - ☐ **c.** energy is needed only during exercise.

2. To get energy to play ball after school, you should
   - ☐ **a.** eat enough candy.
   - ☐ **b.** ride your bike.
   - ☐ **c.** have a healthful lunch.

3. It takes the least amount of energy to ride a bike
   - ☐ **a.** down a hill.
   - ☐ **b.** up a hill.
   - ☐ **c.** on a level road.

4. The tire that causes the least friction when it is rolling is a
   - ☐ **a.** bike tire.
   - ☐ **b.** car tire.
   - ☐ **c.** bus tire.

5. You should wear a helmet
   - ☐ **a.** only when you ride your bike in the street.
   - ☐ **b.** every time you ride your bike.
   - ☐ **c.** only when you ride your bike on long trips.

## C. Reading Strategies

### 1. Recognizing Words in Context

Find the word *increases* in the article. One definition below is closest to the meaning of that word. One definition has the opposite or nearly the opposite meaning. The remaining definition has a meaning that has nothing to do with the other two words. Label the definitions **C** for *closest*, **O** for *opposite* or *nearly opposite*, and **U** for *unrelated*.

_____ **a.** obeys the law of gravity

_____ **b.** becomes greater

_____ **c.** becomes less

### 2. Distinguishing Fact from Opinion

Two of the statements below present *facts,* which can be proved. The other statement is an *opinion,* which expresses someone's thoughts or beliefs. Label the statements **F** for *fact* and **O** for *opinion.*

_____ **a.** Riding a bike is fun.

_____ **b.** A bike tire creates friction.

_____ **c.** More force is needed to pedal uphill.

### 3. Making Correct Inferences

Two of the statements below are correct *inferences,* or reasonable guesses, that are based on information in the article. The other statement is an incorrect inference. Label the statements **C** for *correct* inference and **I** for *incorrect* inference.

_____ **a.** Wearing a bike helmet is a good idea.

_____ **b.** The body turns bananas and sandwiches into energy.

_____ **c.** Bikes are better than cars.

### 4. Understanding Main Ideas

One of the statements below expresses the main idea of the article. Another statement is too general, or too broad. The other explains only part of the article; it is too narrow. Label the statements **M** for *main idea,* **B** for *too broad,* and **N** for *too narrow.*

_____ **a.** Energy is needed to ride a bike.

_____ **b.** Bike wheels are lightweight.

_____ **c.** Energy helps us do many things.

### 5. Responding to the Article

Complete the following sentence in your own words:

Before reading "Using Energy to Ride a Bike," I already knew

_____

_____

## D. Expanding Vocabulary

### Content-Area Words

Complete each sentence with a word from the box. Write the missing word on the line.

| gravity | fuel | transfer | cables | energy |
|---------|------|----------|--------|--------|

1. The _____ supported the piano being lowered through a window.

2. She will _____ the keys from one hand to another.

3. The pull of _____ keeps our feet on the ground.

4. Without _____, our car will not run.

5. If you don't eat a healthful meal, you may not have enough _____ for our hike.


### Academic English

In the article "Using Energy to Ride a Bike," you learned that *create* means "to cause to be." *Create* can also mean "to make," as in the following sentence.

   *My sister creates her own unique clothing.*

Complete the sentence below.

1. For my art project, I would like to *create* _____

Now use the word *create* in a sentence of your own.

2. _____

_____

You also learned that *layer* is a noun that means "one thickness laid over or under another." *Layer* can also be a verb that means "to place over another," as in the following sentence.

   *The artist will layer several colors onto the canvas.*

Complete the sentence below.

3. When it is cold, we *layer* T-shirts under sweaters to _____

Now use the word *layer* in two sentences of your own.

4. _____

5. _____

**Talk It Over** Share your new sentences with a partner.

# Animals of the Forests

## Before You Read

 **Think about what you know.** Read the title and the first two sentences of the article on the opposite page. What do you know about forests? How many kinds of forests can you name?

### Vocabulary

The content-area and academic English words below appear in "Animals of the Forests." Read the definitions and the example sentences.

#### Content-Area Words

**temperate** (tem′pər it) maintaining a mild temperature
> *Example:* People travel to *temperate* areas because they do not like extreme weather.

**tropical** (trop′i kəl) found in or typical of a place that has consistently warm weather
> *Example:* *Tropical* islands have warm weather and a lot of rain.

**equator** (i kwā′tər) an imaginary line circling Earth halfway between the North and South Poles
> *Example:* Places on the *equator* are the same distance from both the North and South Poles.

**canopy** (kan′ə pē) overhead shelter or covering
> *Example:* A bed may have a *canopy* of cloth above it.

**deciduous** (di sij′o͞o əs) known for shedding its leaves every year
> *Example:* *Deciduous* trees, such as oak, shed their leaves in the fall.

#### Academic English

**environments** (en vī′rən mənts) the world around a plant or an animal that affects its life and growth
> *Example:* Caring for Earth's natural *environments* protects people, animals, and plants.

**available** (ə vā′lə bəl) possible to have or find
> *Example:* Water is not *available* in dry areas such as deserts.

Rate each vocabulary word according to the following scale. Write a number next to each content-area and academic English word.

4    I have never seen the word before.

3    I have seen the word but do not know what it means.

2    I know what the word means when I read it.

1    I use the word myself in speaking or writing.

**Dictionary** Now skim the article and look for other words that are new to you. Write each new word and its definition in the Personal Dictionary.

# While You Read

**Tip!** **Think about why you read.** The forests of Earth are home to many amazing animals. Why do different animals live in different kinds of forests? As you read, try to find the answer.

## ANIMALS of the Forests

1   Forests provide habitats, or living **environments,** for many animals. Some of these environments are tropical rain forests, **temperate** rain forests, and deciduous forests.

**Tropical** rain forests are hot and wet. They are hot because they are near the
5   **equator.** They are wet because it rains a lot there—more than 250 centimeters (100 inches) per year. Tropical rain forests have tall evergreen trees covered with thick leafy growths made up of vines and moss. Throughout all levels of the tropical rain forest, there are also thousands of kinds of insects.

The tallest trees are known as emergents because they emerge, or come out,
10   from above the tops of the tall trees. Eagles make their nests here and fly down to catch birds or small monkeys from lower treetops.

The **canopy,** or roof, of the forest is made up of the tops of the tall trees. Fruits, nuts, seeds, and leaves are **available** here. These things are food for many animals, including bats, parrots, and sloths. Some animals drink water from plants
15   shaped like bowls.

Below the canopy is the understory, made up of bushes and the lower parts of trees. Here monkeys with long arms swing from tree to tree. Flying squirrels and frogs jump between tree limbs. Snakes, birds, and jaguars also live here.

The lowest part of the rain forest is the floor. It is dark and covered with dead
20   plants. Rodents, such as mice, hide here. Bigger animals, such as the tapir, which looks a little like a wild pig, use their snouts, or noses, to dig for roots.

Like tropical rain forests, temperate rain forests are wet and have tall trees. Temperate rain forests are found along the western coasts of North America and South America. They are cooler than the tropical forests, so different kinds of
25   plants and animals live there. Some animals, such as owls and opossums, live in the trees. Others—such as deer, bears, frogs, and skunks—live on the forest floor. Unlike tropical rain forests, temperate rain forests have mostly one type of tree.

Another kind of forest is the temperate **deciduous** forest. Trees here do not grow so tall because less rain falls here than in the rain forest. Certain animals
30   that live in the temperate rain forest can be found here too. Some of these are deer, bears, and frogs. Rain forests have evergreen trees, but the trees in deciduous forests lose their leaves in the fall. The animals here have to survive cold winters. Some, such as bears and snakes, hibernate; they spend the winter in a state much like sleep. Others—such as robins, geese, and monarch butterflies—fly to a
35   warmer place for the winter.

**LANGUAGE CONNECTION**

Many plural words end in *s*. Underline the names of animals in the article whose plural form ends in *s*.

**CONTENT CONNECTION**

Can you name one difference between a deciduous forest and a rain forest?

# After You Read

## A. Organizing Ideas

**What do you know about the tropical rain forest?** Create a picture in the frame below that shows the position of the three regions of the rain forest. Create your own way to show how the levels differ.

How are the regions of the tropical rain forest different from one another? Write three or more sentences that describe some of those differences. Did creating the picture help you understand the differences? How?

_____

_____

_____

_____

_____

_____

_____

## B. Comprehension Skills

**Tip!** **Think about how to find answers.** Look back at different parts of the text. What facts help you figure out how to complete the sentences?

Mark box **a, b,** or **c** with an **X** before the choice that best completes each sentence.

### Recalling Facts

1. Tropical rain forests are
   - ☐ **a.** hot and wet.
   - ☐ **b.** cool and wet.
   - ☐ **c.** hot and dry.

2. Jaguars live in
   - ☐ **a.** temperate deciduous forests.
   - ☐ **b.** temperate rain forests.
   - ☐ **c.** tropical rain forests.

3. The rain forest canopy consists of
   - ☐ **a.** shrubs.
   - ☐ **b.** the tops of tall trees.
   - ☐ **c.** the emergents.

4. Temperate rain forests are
   - ☐ **a.** wet and have tall trees.
   - ☐ **b.** found near the equator.
   - ☐ **c.** hot.

5. Deciduous forests are
   - ☐ **a.** found mostly along mild coasts.
   - ☐ **b.** drier than rain forests.
   - ☐ **c.** habitats for monkeys.

### Understanding Ideas

1. From the article, you can conclude that the different kinds of forests
   - ☐ **a.** provide different kinds of animal habitat.
   - ☐ **b.** have the same kinds of animals.
   - ☐ **c.** are found in the same parts of the world.

2. It is likely that the fruit and leaves on the rain forest floor
   - ☐ **a.** fell from the trees above.
   - ☐ **b.** grew on the ground.
   - ☐ **c.** were planted.

3. It is most likely to snow in a
   - ☐ **a.** tropical rain forest.
   - ☐ **b.** temperate deciduous forest.
   - ☐ **c.** temperate rain forest.

4. From the article, you can conclude that robins
   - ☐ **a.** are afraid of opossums.
   - ☐ **b.** live in the same place year round.
   - ☐ **c.** cannot survive in cold weather.

5. In the rain forest, the water in bowl-shaped plants is most likely to come from
   - ☐ **a.** the plants themselves.
   - ☐ **b.** dead leaves.
   - ☐ **c.** rain.

## C. Reading Strategies

### 1. Recognizing Words in Context

Find the word *emergents* in the article. One definition below is closest to the meaning of that word. One definition has the opposite or nearly the opposite meaning. The remaining definition has a meaning that has nothing to do with the other two words. Label the definitions **C** for *closest,* **O** for *opposite* or *nearly opposite,* and **U** for *unrelated.*

_____ **a.** tallest trees

_____ **b.** tallest canopy

_____ **c.** shortest trees

### 2. Distinguishing Fact from Opinion

Two of the statements below present *facts,* which can be proved. The other statement is an *opinion,* which expresses someone's thoughts or beliefs. Label the statements **F** for *fact* and **O** for *opinion.*

_____ **a.** Deciduous forests have trees that lose their leaves.

_____ **b.** Tropical rain forests are prettier than temperate rain forests.

_____ **c.** Fruits, nuts, seeds, and leaves grow in the canopy.

### 3. Making Correct Inferences

Two of the statements below are correct *inferences,* or reasonable guesses, that are based on information in the article. The other statement is an incorrect inference. Label the statements **C** for *correct* inference and **I** for *incorrect* inference.

_____ **a.** Zebras often live in tropical rain forests.

_____ **b.** Animals visit the canopy to find food and water.

_____ **c.** Different plants and animals live in different kinds of forests.

### 4. Understanding Main Ideas

One of the statements below expresses the main idea of the article. Another statement is too general, or too broad. The other explains only part of the article; it is too narrow. Label the statements **M** for *main idea,* **B** for *too broad,* and **N** for *too narrow.*

_____ **a.** A tapir uses its snout to dig for roots.

_____ **b.** Different kinds of forests provide homes for many kinds of plants and animals.

_____ **c.** Every animal has a habitat.

### 5. Responding to the Article

Complete the following sentence in your own words:

Reading "Animals of the Forests" made me want to learn more about

_____

because _____

## D. Expanding Vocabulary

### Content-Area Words

Cross out one word or phrase in each row that is not related to the word in dark type.

| | | | | |
|---|---|---|---|---|
| 1. **equator** | middle | imaginary | overhead | halfway |
| 2. **tropical** | hot | hibernate | rain | emergents |
| 3. **temperate** | different seasons | parrots | tall trees | Americas |
| 4. **deciduous** | leaves that fall | cold winters | birds | humid |
| 5. **canopy** | roof | parrot | seeds | tapir |

### Academic English

In the article "Animals of the Forests," you learned that *environments* are "the world around a plant or an animal that affects its life and growth." *Environments* may be natural, like the forests. *Environments* may also be other surroundings, as in the following sentence.

> *My school has teachers who create exciting classroom environments.*

Complete the sentence below.

**1.** I spend my day in different *environments,* such as home, school, and _____

Now use the word *environments* in a sentence of your own.

**2.** _____

_____

You also learned that *available* means "possible to have or find." *Available* can also mean "usable," as in the following sentence.

> *The red tomatoes in my garden are now available for cooking.*

Complete the sentence below.

**3.** The pizza is now baked and *available* to _____

Now use the word *available* in two sentences of your own.

**4.** _____

**5.** _____

 Share your new sentences with a partner.

## Before You Read

**Think about what you know.** Read the title and the first sentence of the article on the opposite page. What do you predict that the article will be about? What do you know about the constellations?

## Vocabulary

The content-area and academic English words below appear in "The Constellations." Read the definitions and the example sentences.

### Content-Area Words

**stars** (stärz) celestial bodies that appear as bright points of light in the night sky
> *Example:* You can see *stars* shining at night when there are no clouds.

**myths** (miths) traditional stories about gods and heroes that express beliefs
> *Example:* My favorite *myth* is about a hero who rescued people from monsters.

**constellations** (kon′ste lā′shənz) groups of stars often named after characters or objects in myths
> *Example:* The bright North Star is part of a *constellation* called the Big Dipper.

**dipper** (dip′ər) a long-handled cup or bowl used for scooping up liquids
> *Example:* I used a *dipper* to serve bowls of soup to my guests.

**direction** (di rek′shən) a line or path along which something moves, faces, or lies
> *Example:* You might get lost if you turned your car in the wrong *direction*.

### Academic English

**major** (mā′jər) great or large
> *Example:* Interstate highways are *major* roads that cross the United States.

**minor** (mī′nər) small
> *Example:* Elena is the leader of our group; everyone else has a *minor* assignment.

Answer the questions below about the content-area and academic English words. Write your answers in the spaces provided. The first one has been done for you.

1. What word goes with *something you might read from a book?* _____myths_____
2. What word goes with *north, south, east, and west?* _____
3. What word goes with *tiny* or *little?* _____
4. What word goes with *a tool you use when taking water from a bucket?* _____
5. What word goes with *big* or *huge?* _____
6. What word goes with *groups of natural lights in the evening sky?* _____
7. What word goes with *bright lights in the sky?* _____

**Dictionary** Now skim the article and look for other words that are new to you. Write each new word and its definition in the Personal Dictionary.

# While You Read

**Think about why you read.** Have you ever tried to find different constellations in the night sky? List the constellations you have seen. As you read, look for information about those constellations.

# The Constellations

1    From the beginning of time, people have been watching the sky. People long ago saw that certain groups of **stars** appeared in parts of the sky at different times of the year. Farmers used these groups to tell what season it was and when to plant their crops. People used their imagination to name the groups. They
5    named them for animals, gods, objects, and characters from **myths.** These groups of stars are called **constellations.**

One well-known constellation is Orion (the Hunter). It can be seen in North America on winter nights. In the southern part of the constellation are three bright stars in a straight row. These make up Orion's belt. From the belt, other stars reach
10    outward to form a dagger, a kind of knife. At the shoulder is a bright star known as Betelgeuse. Orion's left foot is a star called Rigel.

A constellation that is easy to find is Ursa **Major,** or the Great Bear. The Great Bear can be seen year round in the northern sky. It can be found by first finding the Big Dipper. Four stars make up the bowl of the **dipper.** A line of stars makes
15    up the handle. The bowl of the dipper forms a saddle on the back of the Great Bear. The handle of the dipper is the Great Bear's tail. Before the Civil War, a well-known song spoke of the Big Dipper as the "Drinking Gourd," because both dippers and dried gourds (dipper-shaped vegetables) were commonly used to hold drinking water. Enslaved people who tried to escape followed the Big Dipper to be
20    sure they were going north.

The two stars at the pouring end of the Big Dipper are called pointer stars. This is because they point to the North Star. The North Star, also called Polaris, lies in the same **direction** as the North Pole. Sailors and other people who traveled could always use the North Star to tell them which way north was.

25    The North Star is part of a constellation called Ursa **Minor,** or the Little Bear. Part of the Little Bear is a group of stars called the Little Dipper. The bowl of the dipper is the Little Bear's side, and the handle is the Little Bear's tail. The North Star is at the tip of the tail.

Many more constellations are named for animals. Orion's dogs, Canis Major
30    and Canis Minor, for example, are said to hunt Lepus (the Rabbit) and Taurus (the Bull).

**LANGUAGE CONNECTION**

The idiom *year round* means "all through the year." For example, in a warm climate, people can swim outside year round. What activities can you do year round where you live?

**CONTENT CONNECTION**

The word *canine* means "of the dog family." What, then, do you think the names *Canis Major* and *Canis Minor* mean?

# After You Read

## A. Organizing Ideas

**How has knowledge of the stars helped people?** Complete the web below. How have people used their knowledge about the stars? Scan the article to find three examples. Write down one example in each circle. In the square, write down one example that tells how knowledge of the stars could help you.

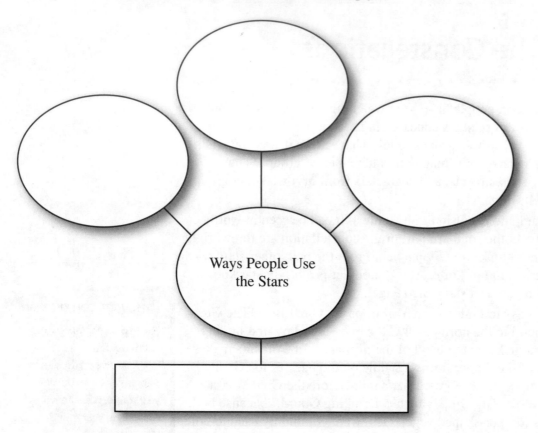

Ways People Use the Stars

Do you think that recognizing the constellations has been useful to people? Write two or more sentences about how things might be different if people had never named or studied the constellations. How did completing the web above help you come to those conclusions?

_____

_____

_____

_____

_____

_____

## B. Comprehension Skills

**Tip!** **Think about how to find answers.** Look back at what you read. The information is in the text, but you may have to look in several sentences to find it.

Mark box **a, b,** or **c** with an **X** before the choice that best completes each sentence.

### Recalling Facts

1. Constellations are
   - ☐ **a.** planets.
   - ☐ **b.** studies of the skies.
   - ☐ **c.** groups of stars.

2. *Ursa Major* means
   - ☐ **a.** "Great Day."
   - ☐ **b.** "Great Bear."
   - ☐ **c.** "Little Bear."

3. *Drinking Gourd* refers to
   - ☐ **a.** the Big Dipper.
   - ☐ **b.** Orion.
   - ☐ **c.** the Little Dipper.

4. Another name for the North Star is
   - ☐ **a.** Orion.
   - ☐ **b.** Lepus.
   - ☐ **c.** Polaris.

5. Lepus and Taurus were named for
   - ☐ **a.** characters from myths.
   - ☐ **b.** animals.
   - ☐ **c.** gods.

### Understanding Ideas

1. From the article, you can conclude that the constellations
   - ☐ **a.** always stay in the same places in the sky.
   - ☐ **b.** were interesting to ancient people.
   - ☐ **c.** are all found in the northern sky.

2. It is most likely that ancient people named many constellations for animals because they
   - ☐ **a.** imagined that the constellations looked like the animals they knew.
   - ☐ **b.** did not like animals.
   - ☐ **c.** were afraid of the stars.

3. From the article, you can conclude that the Big Dipper
   - ☐ **a.** is a very bright star.
   - ☐ **b.** is part of the Great Bear.
   - ☐ **c.** was named after a song.

4. You are most likely to find the North Star by
   - ☐ **a.** following the pointer stars in the Big Dipper.
   - ☐ **b.** first finding Orion's belt.
   - ☐ **c.** looking in the bowl of the Big Dipper.

5. It is most likely that *Canis Major* means
   - ☐ **a.** "Great Dog."
   - ☐ **b.** "Little Dog."
   - ☐ **c.** "Big Bull."

## C. Reading Strategies

### 1. Recognizing Words in Context

Find the word *winter* in the article. One definition below is closest to the meaning of that word. One definition has the opposite or nearly the opposite meaning. The remaining definition has a meaning that has nothing to do with the other two words. Label the definitions **C** for *closest,* **O** for *opposite* or *nearly opposite,* and **U** for *unrelated.*

_____ **a.** summer

_____ **b.** cold season

_____ **c.** breeze

### 2. Distinguishing Fact from Opinion

Two of the statements below present *facts,* which can be proved. The other statement is an *opinion,* which expresses someone's thoughts or beliefs. Label the statements **F** for *fact* and **O** for *opinion.*

_____ **a.** Four stars make up the bowl of the Big Dipper.

_____ **b.** Farmers studied constellations to help them plant crops.

_____ **c.** Taurus (the Bull) is a frightening constellation.

### 3. Making Correct Inferences

Two of the statements below are correct *inferences,* or reasonable guesses, that are based on information in the article. The other statement is an incorrect inference. Label the statements **C** for *correct* inference and **I** for *incorrect* inference.

_____ **a.** Some constellations are easy to find in the night sky if you know their shapes.

_____ **b.** Polaris may help someone tell which way is north.

_____ **c.** The constellations are all named after famous people.

### 4. Understanding Main Ideas

One of the statements below expresses the main idea of the article. Another statement is too general, or too broad. The other explains only part of the article; it is too narrow. Label the statements **M** for *main idea,* **B** for *too broad,* and **N** for *too narrow.*

_____ **a.** Constellations have had an important role throughout history.

_____ **b.** Constellations are groups of stars.

_____ **c.** Many constellations are named after animals.

### 5. Responding to the Article

Complete the following sentence in your own words:

One of the things I did best while reading "The Constellations" was

_____

I think that I did this well because _____

_____

## D. Expanding Vocabulary

### Content-Area Words

Read each item carefully. Write on the line the word or phrase that best completes each sentence.

1. When we looked closely at the _____, we could see the constellations.

    sky                    myths                    dipper

2. The bowl of the Big Dipper is made up of four _____.

    stars                  belts                    directions

3. Some constellations, such as Orion (the Hunter), were named after _____ in myths.

    directions             daggers                  characters

4. The saddle on the back of the _____ constellation is shaped like a dipper.

    Little Bear            Great Bear               Orion

5. One way enslaved people knew which direction to take was by looking for the

    _____.

    Great Bear            Big Dipper               Betelgeuse star

### Academic English

In the article "The Constellations," you learned that *major* means "great or large." *Major* can also mean "more important than something else," as in the following sentence.

> *Learning is my major goal in school, although I want to play sports too.*

Complete the sentence below.

1. A *major* reason people buy cars is _____

Now use the word *major* in a sentence of your own.

2. _____

You also learned that *minor* is an adjective meaning "small." *Minor* can also be a noun meaning "under full legal age," as in the following sentence.

> *A minor may not marry without the consent of a parent.*

Complete the sentence below.

3. A scratched arm is a *minor* injury compared to _____

Now use the word *minor* in two sentences of your own.

4. _____

5. _____

**Talk It Over** Share your new sentences with a partner.

# Before You Read

**Tip!** **Think about what you know.** Read the lesson title above. Think about what you already know about plants. Why do people need plants? Read the article to find the answers.

## Vocabulary

The content-area and academic English words below appear in "The Need for Plants." Read the definitions and the example sentences.

### Content-Area Words

**grains** (grānz) edible seeds or seedlike fruits of plants such as rye, wheat, or corn
*Example:* Bread made from whole *grains* is healthful.

**cotton** (kot′ən) fluffy fibers that grow in a fluffy mass in large seed pods on certain plants
*Example:* Clothes made from *cotton* fibers are comfortable.

**petroleum** (pə trō′lē əm) a flammable liquid made by nature deep beneath Earth's surface
*Example:* People must drill deep underground to find *petroleum*.

**plastic** (plas′tik) material, made from petroleum, that can be molded or shaped when soft
*Example:* Glass dishes break more easily than *plastic* dishes.

**electricity** (ə lek′ tris′ə tē) energy that is capable of producing light, heat, and other effects
*Example:* Lamps and television sets require *electricity* to work.

### Academic English

**derived** (də rīvd′) obtained or gotten (from something else)
*Example:* People often *derive* great pleasure from music.

**source** (sôrs) place from which something comes
*Example:* The sun is the *source* of heat for Earth.

Read again the example sentences that follow the content-area and academic English word definitions. With a partner, discuss the meanings of the words and sentences.

 Now skim the article and look for other words that are new to you. Write each new word and its definition in the Personal Dictionary.

# While You Read

**Tip!** **Think about why you read.** Think about how you use plants and things made from plants. How many things do you use each day that come from plants? As you read, try to find more ways that you use plants in your life each day.

## The Need for Plants

1   Imagine a world in which there is no cereal for breakfast, no peanut butter and jelly for lunch, and nothing at all for dinner. There are no hamburgers, french fries, or salads. People cannot do, have, or make other basic things. There are no shirts, jeans, hats, socks, or shoes. There are no cars or planes. This is a world
5   without plants.

All of our food comes from plants. Cereals are made from **grains,** which are **derived** from plants. For example, the **source** of oatmeal is oats. Flour—which is used for bread, cakes, and doughnuts—is made from ground wheat. The vegetables we eat, such as carrots and spinach, are the roots and leaves of plants.
10  Oranges, grapes, and pears are fruits that grow on trees or vines. Beef and milk come from cattle, and cattle eat corn and grass. All animals either eat plants or eat other animals that eat plants. So even our Thanksgiving holiday turkeys come to our dinner tables, indirectly, from plants.

Our clothes come from plants. **Cotton** is a plant part that is made into cloth.
15  Cotton is used to make jeans, T-shirts, and other clothes. It is also used for towels, sheets, and some rugs. Another fabric is polyester. Polyester comes from **petroleum.** Petroleum comes from plants and animals that died millions of years ago and decayed beneath the surface of Earth. The buttons on your shirt may be made from tagua nuts, which grow on trees in the rain forest. The heels and
20  soles of your shoes may be rubber that comes from trees.

**Plastic,** too, comes from plants. Like polyester, plastic is created from petroleum. Just think of all those ancient decayed plants that have been turned into plastic bottles, trash bags, clothes hangers, car parts, garbage cans, and dishes! Rope can be made from plastic or from hemp, which is a plant. Many
25  houses are built of wood from trees. Paper is made from wood pulp. Some paint is made from plant oil.

For centuries people have used plants to treat illness. For example, digitalis, which comes from a plant called foxglove, is made into a drug to treat heart problems. Many other medicines are also made from plants.
30  Much of the **electricity** we use to heat and light our homes comes from burning coal and other fuels, which come from plants. Without plants we would be cold and hungry. Without plants it would be impossible for us to live.

### LANGUAGE CONNECTION

Some plurals are irregular. The word *cattle* is a plural form of *cow* and *bull*. *Children* is the plural form of *child*. What other words have irregular plural forms?

### CONTENT CONNECTION

When plants die, they sink into the ground. Over many years, layers of dead plants build up. Pressure turns these layers into coal, a natural fuel. Do you know what coal can turn into with even more pressure and heat?

# After You Read

## A. Organizing Ideas

**How did you use plants today?** Complete the chart below. First, think about what you learned from the article about plants and things that come from plants. Then, in the first column, list things you used today that came from plants. In the second column, explain how those things came from plants. The first one has been done for you.

| What I Used Today | How It Came from a Plant |
|---|---|
| I ate an orange for breakfast. | Oranges grow on trees. |
| | |
| | |
| | |
| | |
| | |
| | |

Were you surprised by how much you have used plants today? Write two or more sentences about what you learned from completing this chart. How did the chart draw your attention to how important the information in the article is to your life?

_____

_____

_____

_____

## B. Comprehension Skills

**Tip!** **Think about how to find answers.** Look back at different parts of the text. Think about the facts that help you figure out how to complete each item.

Mark box **a**, **b**, or **c** with an **X** before the choice that best completes each sentence.

### Recalling Facts

1. Cereals are made from
   - ☐ **a.** vegetables.
   - ☐ **b.** milk.
   - ☐ **c.** grains.

2. Cotton
   - ☐ **a.** grows in the rain forest.
   - ☐ **b.** can be made into fabric.
   - ☐ **c.** is a kind of polyester.

3. Plastic is made from
   - ☐ **a.** petroleum.
   - ☐ **b.** tagua nuts.
   - ☐ **c.** wood.

4. Digitalis is made into a kind of
   - ☐ **a.** medicine.
   - ☐ **b.** plastic.
   - ☐ **c.** math.

5. Without plants we
   - ☐ **a.** would eat meat.
   - ☐ **b.** could not survive.
   - ☐ **c.** would wear polyester.

### Understanding Ideas

1. From the article, you can conclude that beef
   - ☐ **a.** is not connected with plants in any way.
   - ☐ **b.** comes from animals that eat plants.
   - ☐ **c.** tastes better than pork.

2. You can also conclude that
   - ☐ **a.** plants have been on Earth for a long time.
   - ☐ **b.** all plants can be made into clothing.
   - ☐ **c.** all plants are good to eat.

3. It is likely that the clothes you are wearing are made from
   - ☐ **a.** fabrics that were made from plants.
   - ☐ **b.** plants from the rain forest.
   - ☐ **c.** polyester.

4. From the article, you can conclude that plastic is
   - ☐ **a.** made from rubber.
   - ☐ **b.** used to make many useful things.
   - ☐ **c.** used to make medicines.

5. You can also conclude that
   - ☐ **a.** plants grow mainly in forests.
   - ☐ **b.** fruits taste better than vegetables.
   - ☐ **c.** many kinds of products come from plants.

## C. Reading Strategies

### 1. Recognizing Words in Context

Find the word *decayed* in the article. One definition below is closest to the meaning of that word. One definition has the opposite or nearly the opposite meaning. The remaining definition has a meaning that has nothing to do with the other two words. Label the definitions **C** for *closest,* **O** for *opposite* or *nearly opposite,* and **U** for *unrelated.*

_____ **a.** grew

_____ **b.** discovered

_____ **c.** rotted

### 2. Distinguishing Fact from Opinion

Two of the statements below present *facts,* which can be proved. The other statement is an *opinion,* which expresses someone's thoughts or beliefs. Label the statements **F** for *fact* and **O** for *opinion.*

_____ **a.** Polyester is made from petroleum.

_____ **b.** Flour and oatmeal are both made from grains.

_____ **c.** Digitalis is the best medicine for people with heart problems.

### 3. Making Correct Inferences

Two of the statements below are correct *inferences,* or reasonable guesses, that are based on information in the article. The other statement is an incorrect inference. Label the statements **C** for *correct* inference and **I** for *incorrect* inference.

_____ **a.** Things we use every day exist because of plants.

_____ **b.** Plants play a role in almost every food we eat.

_____ **c.** We can build houses using materials other than wood.

### 4. Understanding Main Ideas

One of the statements below expresses the main idea of the article. Another statement is too general, or too broad. The other explains only part of the article; it is too narrow. Label the statements **M** for *main idea,* **B** for *too broad,* and **N** for *too narrow.*

_____ **a.** Many medicines are made from plants.

_____ **b.** Without plants, people could not live.

_____ **c.** Plants are good for our planet.

### 5. Responding to the Article

Complete the following sentence in your own words:

What interested me most in "The Need for Plants" was

_____

_____

## D. Expanding Vocabulary

### Content-Area Words

Complete each analogy with a word from the box. Write in the missing word.

| cotton | petroleum | grains | plastic | electricity |

**1.** milk : cheese :: _____ : cereal

**2.** digitalis : foxglove :: _____ : petroleum

**3.** plastic : hemp :: polyester : _____

**4.** gasoline : car :: _____ : television

**5.** tagua nuts : rain forest :: _____ : beneath the earth

### Academic English

In the article "The Need for Plants," you learned that *derived* means "obtained or gotten (from something else)." *Derived* can also mean "traced back to an earlier form," as in the following sentence.

*The word* computer *is derived from the Latin word* computare, *which means "to count up or to add."*

Complete the sentence below.

**1.** Many English words are *derived* from other languages, such as Greek or _____

Now use the word *derived* in a sentence of your own.

**2.** _____

_____

You also learned that *source* means "place from which something comes." *Source* can also mean "the beginning," as in the following sentence.

*The source of the river is in the mountains.*

Complete the sentence below.

**3.** Fire can be a *source* of _____

Now use the word *source* in two sentences of your own.

**4.** _____

**5.** _____

Share your new sentences with a partner.

# Before You Read

**Tip!** **Think about what you know.** Read the first and last sentences of the article on the opposite page. What do you know about how veterinarians take care of animals? Have you ever seen a veterinarian work?

## Vocabulary

The content-area and academic English words below appear in "What Is a Veterinarian?" Read the definitions and the example sentences.

### Content-Area Words

**veterinarian** (vet′ər ə nãr′ē ən) a doctor who is trained to care for animals
*Example:* I take my pets to a *veterinarian* when they are sick.

**patients** (pā′shənts) people or animals that are helped by a doctor or a veterinarian
*Example:* Doctors help their *patients* stay healthy.

**surgery** (sur′jər ē) removal or repair of a part of the body
*Example:* I needed *surgery* to repair my broken leg.

**tumors** (tōō′mərz) growths in the body that form when the number of normal body cells increases too quickly
*Example:* The lumps on the dog's leg were *tumors*.

**injuries** (in′jər ēz) damage to the body of a person or an animal
*Example:* A car accident can result in *injuries* to the driver, passengers, and people nearby.

### Academic English

**remove** (ri mōōv′) to take away
*Example:* A pencil eraser can help you *remove* mistakes in writing.

**requires** (ri kwīrz′) makes necessary
*Example:* A cook *requires* sugar to make a chocolate cake.

Rate each vocabulary word according to the following scale. Write a number next to each content-area and academic English word.

4    I have never seen the word before.

3    I have seen the word but do not know what it means.

2    I know what the word means when I read it.

1    I use the word myself in speaking or writing.

 Now skim the article and look for other words that are new to you. Write each new word and its definition in the Personal Dictionary.

# While You Read

**Tip!** **Think about why you read.** Do you have a pet, or have you seen animals on a farm? As you read, look for different ways that veterinarians help animals stay healthy.

## What Is a Veterinarian?

1  A **veterinarian** is an animal doctor. Veterinarians are also called vets. They treat animals that are sick or hurt, and they help healthy animals stay well.

Some vets treat small animals, such as cats, dogs, birds, and hamsters. Many vets who treat small animals work at pet clinics. People bring their pets in to see 5 vets. Vets give checkups to **patients** that seem healthy. Suppose the patient is a dog. The vet looks at the dog's fur and skin. The vet does this to check for fleas or skin problems. The vet looks into the dog's ears and at its teeth. Then the vet checks the inside of the dog by feeling its internal body parts through the skin.

Vets also teach pet owners how to take care of their pets. Vets keep pets from 10 getting sick by giving them shots or other protective medicine. They clean their patients' teeth and perform **surgery.** One kind of surgery is to spay or neuter dogs and cats to prevent them from having unwanted puppies or kittens. Vets also operate to **remove tumors.** They repair broken bones and other **injuries.**

Some vets treat farm animals, such as horses, cows, sheep, pigs, goats, and 15 chickens. These vets go to farms to see their patients. Vets must carry all of their supplies with them. They may need to test a herd of cattle for sickness. In fact, they may give a shot to every animal in the herd. Vets may help a horse give birth to a foal or stitch a cut on a pig's leg. They may even perform surgery in a barn.

Other vets take care of zoo animals. A zoo vet has to treat many kinds of 20 animals. These can include fish, bears, snakes, and seals. Zoo vets might give a zebra a checkup or operate on an elephant. They might clean a lion's teeth or trim a bird's claws. Before working on large zoo animals, vets first make them fall asleep. They do this by shooting tiny pointed objects called darts into the animals' bodies. The darts contain medicine that puts them to sleep. When the vet finishes 25 working on an animal, he or she may give the animal a shot to wake it up.

Becoming a vet **requires** years of school. First, students must take college classes. Then they must go to a school of veterinary medicine and earn a Doctor of Veterinary Medicine degree. All vets also have one thing in common. They care about animals.

**LANGUAGE CONNECTION**

*Vet* is the short form of the word *veterinarian*. Why do you think a short form of the word is useful?

**CONTENT CONNECTION**

The last paragraph explains two ideas. First, vets must study for many years. Second, vets must care about animals. What other jobs require people to study for many years and care about others?

# After You Read

## A. Organizing Ideas

**How do veterinarians help animals?** Complete the chart below. First, think about what veterinarians do. Use the article to help you. Read the headings How Vets Keep Animals Healthy and How Vets Help Sick Animals. List examples below each heading. The first one has been done for you.

| How Vets Keep Animals Healthy | How Vets Help Sick Animals |
|---|---|
| checking animals for fleas | operating to remove tumors |
| | |
| | |
| | |
| | |
| | |
| | |

Did completing the chart help you think about what vets do? Write two or more sentences about the usefulness of the chart. Do you think that you would like to be a veterinarian someday? Did completing the chart help you know whether you would be interested in being a vet?

_____

_____

_____

## B. Comprehension Skills

**Tip!** **Think about how to find answers.** Think about what each item means. Try to say it to yourself in your own words before you complete it.

Mark box **a, b,** or **c** with an **X** before the choice that best completes each sentence.

### Recalling Facts

1. Veterinarians are
   - ☐ **a.** farmers.
   - ☐ **b.** zookeepers.
   - ☐ **c.** animal doctors.

2. Part of a veterinarian's job is to
   - ☐ **a.** treat animals that are sick.
   - ☐ **b.** raise farm animals.
   - ☐ **c.** go to school.

3. Veterinarians spay or neuter cats in order to
   - ☐ **a.** give them shots.
   - ☐ **b.** give them checkups.
   - ☐ **c.** prevent them from having unwanted kittens.

4. Part of a zoo veterinarian's job may be to
   - ☐ **a.** clean a bear's teeth.
   - ☐ **b.** give farm animals checkups.
   - ☐ **c.** give shots to people's pets.

5. To become a veterinarian, a student must first
   - ☐ **a.** become a Doctor of Veterinary Medicine.
   - ☐ **b.** visit zoos and farms.
   - ☐ **c.** own dogs and cats.

### Understanding Ideas

1. A vet who treats small animals may
   - ☐ **a.** give a pet rabbit a checkup.
   - ☐ **b.** help an antelope give birth.
   - ☐ **c.** treat a sick cow.

2. From the article, you can conclude that a vet who gives a dog a checkup
   - ☐ **a.** gives the dog a quick look.
   - ☐ **b.** examines every part of the dog's body.
   - ☐ **c.** performs surgery on the dog.

3. You can also conclude that vets
   - ☐ **a.** like animals more than people.
   - ☐ **b.** sometimes save animals' lives.
   - ☐ **c.** have to visit zoos.

4. It is most likely that vets who treat farm animals carry along
   - ☐ **a.** overalls.
   - ☐ **b.** medicine.
   - ☐ **c.** saddles.

5. A zoo vet is most likely to treat a sick
   - ☐ **a.** camel.
   - ☐ **b.** pet cat.
   - ☐ **c.** chicken.

## C. Reading Strategies

### 1. Recognizing Words in Context

Find the word *treat* in the article. One definition below is closest to the meaning of that word. One definition has the opposite or nearly the opposite meaning. The remaining definition has a meaning that has nothing to do with the other two words. Label the definitions **C** for *closest*, **O** for *opposite* or *nearly opposite*, and **U** for *unrelated*.

_____ **a.** care for

_____ **b.** injure

_____ **c.** build

### 2. Distinguishing Fact from Opinion

Two of the statements below present *facts*, which can be proved. The other statement is an *opinion*, which expresses someone's thoughts or beliefs. Label the statements **F** for *fact* and **O** for *opinion*.

_____ **a.** Zoo vets make their patients fall asleep before working on them.

_____ **b.** Veterinarians are smarter than dentists.

_____ **c.** Vets care for healthy and sick animals.

### 3. Making Correct Inferences

Two of the statements below are correct *inferences*, or reasonable guesses, that are based on information in the article. The other statement is an incorrect inference. Label the statements **C** for *correct* inference and **I** for *incorrect* inference.

_____ **a.** It is safer for a zoo vet to work on a sleeping animal than on one that is awake.

_____ **b.** A veterinarian may help a dog give birth to puppies.

_____ **c.** Some cats bite veterinarians.

### 4. Understanding Main Ideas

One of the statements below expresses the main idea of the article. Another statement is too general, or too broad. The other explains only part of the article; it is too narrow. Label the statements **M** for *main idea*, **B** for *too broad*, and **N** for *too narrow*.

_____ **a.** Vets treat healthy and unhealthy animals for many reasons.

_____ **b.** Vets check a dog's skin and fur for problems.

_____ **c.** Veterinarians are animal doctors.

### 5. Responding to the Article

Complete the following sentence in your own words:

One thing in "What Is a Veterinarian?" that I cannot understand is

_____

_____

_____

## D. Expanding Vocabulary

### Content-Area Words

Cross out one word or phrase in each row that is not related to the word in dark type.

| 1. | **injuries** | hurt | treat | healthy | bandage |
|---|---|---|---|---|---|
| 2. | **patients** | dog | zebra | cow | truck |
| 3. | **surgery** | pills | spay | tumors | bones |
| 4. | **tumors** | growth | tooth | disease | body |
| 5. | **veterinarian** | animals | doctor | college | library |

### Academic English

In the article "What Is a Veterinarian?" you learned that *remove* means "to take away." *Remove* can also mean "dismiss" or "fire," as in the following sentence.

*The coach will remove the athlete from the game for breaking the rules.*

Complete the sentence below.

1. An employer might *remove* an employee from a job because _____

Now use the word *remove* in a sentence of your own.

2. _____

_____

You also learned that *requires* means "makes necessary." *Requires* can also mean "commands or orders," as in the following sentence.

*The teacher requires your assignments to be neat and on time.*

Complete the sentence below.

3. A red light *requires* cars to _____

Now use the word *requires* in two sentences of your own.

4. _____

5. _____

Talk It Over   Share your new sentences with a partner.

## Writing a Postcard

Read the postcard. Then complete the sentences. Use words from the Word Bank.

Dear Jamina,

    Hello from Central America! We are near the
(1) _____, where it is always hot and wet.
Today we walked far into the (2) _____ forest.
I looked up at the tops of the trees and saw many
colorful birds in the branches. Then I looked in another
(3) _____. On the forest floor, I saw rodents,
tapirs, and insects. Birds, animals, and insects make their
homes in different (4) _____ in the forest. Last
night we went to a festival in a small town. We heard a
storyteller tell (5) _____ from long ago about
how the forest and people came to be here. I'll show you
photos as soon as I get home!

                          Damir

**Word Bank**
myths
equator
tropical
direction
environments

Jamina Krukec
1431 Main Street
Hometown
Home State 12345
U.S.A.

## Reading an Advertisement

Read the advertisement. Circle the word that completes each sentence.

# Visit to a Space Center

### Visit a space center! You will be with space workers for a day! Here is what you can see!

- Watch engineers work on new space flights. They must **(create, layer)** the plans for each trip into space.

- Go to the control room. An important spaceship is going to take off, or launch. Listen to everyone cheer as this **(major, fuel)** space trip starts.

- Look at the computer screens. Think about what happens to the spaceship. It leaves Earth. Then it goes through each **(layer, fuel)** of the atmosphere.

- Learn how the spaceship uses supplies and **(major, fuel)** to travel long distances from Earth.

- Put on a spacesuit and enter a special room. You will feel very light, as if you are walking on the moon. The room has no **(gravity, layer)**.

### Will you fly into space someday?

**Making Connections**

Work with a partner. Talk about what the words mean. How can you use the words to talk about a car? List your ideas in the outline of the car below.

| remove | derived | minor | source | available |
|--------|---------|-------|--------|-----------|
| electricity | plastic | cables | energy | requires |

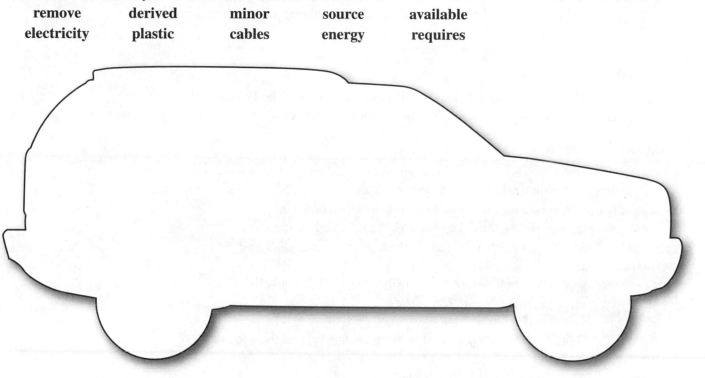

Use all of the words above in complete sentences of your own. Each sentence may include one or more of the words. To help you start writing, look at the ideas you wrote about. After you write your sentences, read them over. If you find a mistake, correct it.

_____

_____

_____

_____

_____

_____

_____

_____

_____

_____

## Before You Read

**Tip!** **Think about what you know.** Read the title of the lesson. What do you predict the article will be about? What do you already know about Earth's surface?

## Vocabulary

The content-area and academic English words below appear in "The Features of Earth's Surface." Read the definitions and the example sentences.

### Content-Area Words

**lithosphere** (lith′ə sfēr′) the layer of rock on which all of Earth's land and oceans rest
*Example:* The *lithosphere* is covered by land or water.

**plates** (plāts) huge pieces of rock that make up the landmasses on Earth
*Example:* Earthquakes are caused by the movements of Earth's *plates.*

**volcanoes** (vol kā′ nōz) holes in Earth's surface through which lava, gases, and rocks erupt
*Example:* *Volcanoes* sometimes shoot hot melted rock and gases into the air.

**magma** (mag′mə) melted rock beneath Earth's surface
*Example:* *Magma* that explodes from a volcano is called lava.

**erosion** (i rō′zhən) the slow wearing or washing away, smoothing, and shaping of soil and rock
*Example:* *Erosion* made the large rock smaller and smoother.

### Academic English

**sections** (sek′shənz) parts that are cut off or separated from other parts
*Example:* At the video store, my friend goes straight to the action movie *section,* while I go to the comedy area.

**occurs** (ə kurz′) appears or happens
*Example:* Thunder sometimes *occurs* during a storm.

Answer the questions below. Circle the part of each question that is the answer. The first one has been done for you.

1. Are the (continents) or the oceans part of Earth's *plates?*
2. Which probably *occurs* more often in the American Southwest, a rainstorm or a sandstorm?
3. Is the *lithosphere* under Earth's surface or above Earth's surface?
4. Which separates the *sections* of a house, the roof or the walls?
5. Does *erosion* change a rock by building it up or wearing it down?
6. Do *volcanoes* build up or wear down Earth's surface?
7. Would you be more likely to find *magma* above the ground or below the ground?

 **Dictionary** Now skim the article and look for other words that are new to you. Write each new word and its definition in the Personal Dictionary.

# While You Read

**Tip!** **Think about why you read.** The surface of Earth is always changing. Can you name one way Earth changes? As you read, think about how you would use this information.

## The Features of Earth's Surface

1    The surface of Earth is wrinkled with mountains and carved out with valleys. In some places the surface is flat. Earth is crossed by rivers and dotted with lakes. Much of it is covered by ocean.

   All of Earth's land and its oceans rest on a layer of rock. This layer is called the
5  **lithosphere.** The lithosphere is made up of **sections** called **plates.** Large cracks, or faults, separate these plates. Plates move because of pressure from deep within Earth. When plates move apart, they can cause large blocks of Earth's surface to sink. When plates press against each other, they can push up layers of rock. Some mountains are created this way.

10    Other mountains are made by **volcanoes.** Melted rock called **magma** moves up from deep inside Earth. As it rises, it gives off gases. These gases push on Earth's surface and cause it to bulge. When the pressure gets very high, the gas explodes from the ground. The magma that shoots out of the volcano is called lava. When the volcano erupts, or releases lava, again and again, the lava builds up to form a
15  mountain. Sometimes many years pass between eruptions.

   Land can also be shaped by **erosion.** Erosion **occurs** when water or wind wears away softer rock and leaves behind harder rock. After a long, long time, the harder rock may stand alone as mountains. Sometimes this hard rock appears as the walls of canyons.

20    Water moves from high ground to low ground. Small streams can come together to form large streams. Large streams can join to form rivers. Rivers flow into lakes or the ocean.

   The ocean is a huge body of salt water that covers almost three-fourths of Earth. The ocean is divided into smaller oceans and seas. On the ocean floor are
25  the mid-ocean ridges, chains of mountains formed by volcanoes. As some of the large cracks between the ridges widen, magma flows up through the cracks and forms new mountains. Many islands are volcanoes that have risen above the surface of the ocean. Hawaii was formed this way. Some of Hawaii's vocanoes are still active, or erupting.

30    The surface of Earth is always changing. At one time, all land was joined together in one place, and the ocean covered the rest of the world. As the plates slowly moved, the land broke apart. Ocean water moved between the masses of land. Over a long period of time, these masses became the continents we know today.

### LANGUAGE CONNECTION

To *give off* means "to pour forth or release something." For example, a fire gives off smoke. Can you think of other ways to use this expression?

### CONTENT CONNECTION

The way continents were formed shows us cause and effect in action. Can you find other examples of cause and effect in this article?

# After You Read

## A. Organizing Ideas

**How do Earth's features change?** Complete the chart below. Think about ways that Earth changes. Use the article to help you. In the first column, list the causes for the changes. In the second column, list the things that have changed and continue to change Earth. The first cause and effect have been done for you.

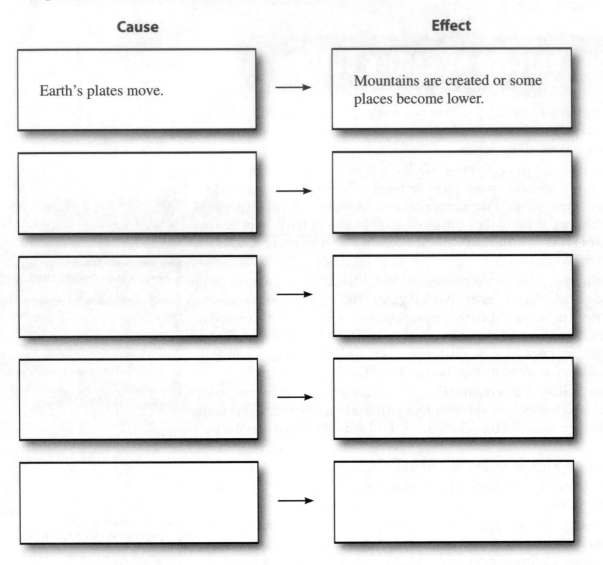

**Cause**                    **Effect**

Earth's plates move. ⟶ Mountains are created or some places become lower.

What did you learn by completing the chart? Write two or more sentences about your ideas. Would you use this type of chart again to organize causes and effects?

_____

_____

_____

## B. Comprehension Skills

**Tip!** **Think about how to find answers.** Look back at what you read. The information is in the text, but you may have to look in several sentences to find it.

Mark box **a, b,** or **c** with an **X** before the choice that best completes each sentence.

### Recalling Facts

1. The lithosphere is
   - ☐ **a.** the bottom of the ocean.
   - ☐ **b.** a layer of rock.
   - ☐ **c.** a volcano.

2. The lithosphere is made up of
   - ☐ **a.** lava.
   - ☐ **b.** mountains.
   - ☐ **c.** plates.

3. Magma is
   - ☐ **a.** melted rock.
   - ☐ **b.** erosion.
   - ☐ **c.** salt water.

4. The ocean covers almost three-fourths of Earth's
   - ☐ **a.** plates.
   - ☐ **b.** surface.
   - ☐ **c.** magma.

5. The mid-ocean ridges
   - ☐ **a.** are mountains under the ocean.
   - ☐ **b.** were formed by erosion.
   - ☐ **c.** are crossed by rivers.

### Understanding Ideas

1. From the article, you can conclude that the surface of Earth
   - ☐ **a.** has stopped changing.
   - ☐ **b.** is continuously sinking.
   - ☐ **c.** is continuously changing.

2. Mountains are most likely to form
   - ☐ **a.** along faults.
   - ☐ **b.** in the middle of a plate.
   - ☐ **c.** next to canyons.

3. From the article, you can conclude that erosion can
   - ☐ **a.** cause a volcano to erupt.
   - ☐ **b.** make a mountain bigger.
   - ☐ **c.** change rock.

4. You can also conclude that
   - ☐ **a.** there is more land than ocean on Earth.
   - ☐ **b.** the ocean will someday cover all of the land.
   - ☐ **c.** there is more ocean than land on Earth.

5. You can also conclude that
   - ☐ **a.** the surface of Earth will continue to change.
   - ☐ **b.** the continents will remain where they are.
   - ☐ **c.** volcanoes do not change Earth's surface.

## C. Reading Skills

### 1. Recognizing Words in Context

Find the word *wrinkled* in the article. One definition below is closest to the meaning of that word. One definition has the opposite or nearly the opposite meaning. The remaining definition has a meaning that has nothing to do with the other two words. Label the definitions **C** for *closest*, **O** for *opposite* or *nearly opposite*, and **U** for *unrelated*.

_____ **a.** smooth

_____ **b.** bumpy

_____ **c.** shiny

### 2. Distinguishing Fact from Opinion

Two of the statements below present *facts,* which can be proved. The other statement is an *opinion,* which expresses someone's thoughts or beliefs. Label the statements **F** for *fact* and **O** for *opinion*.

_____ **a.** Some mountains are made by volcanoes.

_____ **b.** The ocean contains salt water.

_____ **c.** Lakes are cleaner than oceans.

### 3. Making Correct Inferences

Two of the statements below are correct *inferences,* or reasonable guesses, that are based on information in the article. The other statement is an incorrect inference. Label the statements **C** for *correct* inference and **I** for *incorrect* inference.

_____ **a.** Erosion wears away only rock.

_____ **b.** The lithosphere is still changing.

_____ **c.** Hot lava can be dangerous to animals, people, and buildings.

### 4. Understanding Main Ideas

One of the statements below expresses the main idea of the article. Another statement is too general, or too broad. The other explains only part of the article; it is too narrow. Label the statements **M** for *main idea,* **B** for *too broad,* and **N** for *too narrow.*

_____ **a.** Earth's surface has many features.

_____ **b.** Water and wind shape land through erosion.

_____ **c.** Earth's surface moves, shifts, and changes continuously.

### 5. Responding to the Article

Complete the following sentence in your own words:

Now that I have read "The Features of Earth's Surface," I want to learn more about

_____

because _____

_____

## D. Expanding Vocabulary

### Content-Area Words

Complete each sentence with a word from the box. Write the missing word on the line.

| plates | magma | volcanoes | lithosphere | erosion |

1. Land and water on this planet rest on a layer called the _____ .

2. Earth's surface is slowly shaped over time by _____ .

3. Earth's _____ move and shift continuously.

4. _____ is hot melted rock found below the surface of Earth.

5. Islands such as Hawaii were formed from _____ that erupted from the bottom of the ocean.

### Academic English

In the article "The Features of Earth's Surface," you learned that *sections* is a noun that means "parts that are cut off or separated from other parts." *Sections* can also be a verb meaning "separates into parts," as in the following sentence.

*My mother usually sections a pizza into eight pieces.*

Complete the sentence below.

1. Sometimes a teacher *sections* a class into small discussion _____

Now use the word *sections* in a sentence of your own.

2. _____

_____

You also learned that *occurs* means "appears" or "happens." *Occurs* can also mean "comes to mind," as in the following sentence.

*It occurs to me that I have forgotten my coat.*

Complete the sentence below.

3. When it *occurs* to you that you are lost, you will probably _____

Now use the word *occurs* in two sentences of your own.

4. _____

5. _____

**Share your new sentences with a partner.**

# Before You Read

 **Think about what you know.** Read the title and the first paragraph of the article on the opposite page. What do you already know about simple machines?

## Vocabulary

The content-area and academic English words below appear in "Simple Machines." Read the definitions and the example sentences.

### Content-Area Words

**machine** (mə shēn′) a combination of parts that use forces, motion, and energy to do specialized work
> *Example:* A car is a *machine* that carries people from one place to another.

**lever** (lev′ər) a solid bar used to apply force at one end of something
> *Example:* He pushed down the *lever* to lift the chest.

**fulcrum** (fool′krəm) a support, or point of support, on which a lever rests
> *Example:* The boy's toy lever was supported by a *fulcrum* made of toy logs.

**pulley** (pool′ē) a grooved wheel along which a rope or chain is pulled, often to move heavy loads
> *Example:* The old window opened and closed by means of a rope *pulley*.

**inclined plane** (in klīnd′ plān) any flat, sloped surface
> *Example:* The driveway into the parking garage was an *inclined plane*.

### Academic English

**benefits** (ben′ə fits) is helpful to
> *Example:* School *benefits* students by providing them with skills and knowledge.

**complex** (kəm pleks′) having many related parts that work together
> *Example:* A television set is a *complex* electronic machine.

Read again the example sentences that follow the content-area and academic English word definitions. With a partner, discuss the meanings of the words and sentences.

Now skim the article and look for other words that are new to you. Write each new word and its definition in the Personal Dictionary.

# While You Read

**Tip!** **Think about why you read.** Many people use machines every day. What kinds of machines do you use every day? As you read, think about the times you have used or seen the machines described in the article.

1 A **machine** is something that **benefits** people. It helps them do more work than they can do by themselves. When you think of a machine, you probably think of something **complex** that has many parts. However, some machines have only one or two parts. These are called simple machines. Simple machines make
5 it easier to move heavy objects. Some of the most common simple machines are levers, pulleys, and inclined planes.

A **lever** is a rod or a plank. When using a lever, a person transfers a force from one end of the rod to the other. This is done by putting the rod on a **fulcrum,** a point that does not move. One kind of lever is the seesaw that you might see in a
10 park or on a playground. Here the fulcrum is in the middle. A seat is at each end of the plank, or lever. When one end is pushed down, the weight on the other end is raised. When a fulcrum is close to one end of a lever, very little force is needed at the other end to move the object. Another common example of a lever is a crowbar.

15 Another simple machine is a **pulley.** A pulley has a wheel that turns on an axle. A rope or chain runs through a groove cut into the edge of the wheel. The wheel of the pulley turns when the rope is pulled. Pulleys are often attached at high places, such as on a wood beam on the ceiling of a warehouse. One end of the rope may be tied around an object. When someone pulls on the other end, the
20 wheel changes the direction of the force that is created. The pulley makes it easier to lift the object. It is easier to pull down a rope that carries a heavy load than to pull the load up.

An **inclined plane**—a flat, slanted surface, such as a ramp—is also a simple machine. Pushing an object up a ramp is easier than lifting the object straight up.
25 The longer the ramp, the easier it is to move the object. This is because gravity pulls more strongly against something that moves straight up than it does against something that moves on a slant. Another example of an inclined plane is a road going up a hill. The steeper the road is, the more difficult it is to walk up it.

**LANGUAGE CONNECTION**

*Complex* and *simple* are antonyms, words with opposite meanings. Something complex has many parts. Simple things have fewer parts. Can you think of other words that are antonyms?

**CONTENT CONNECTION**

Ramps are inclined planes. Think of ramps that you see in buildings. How do people use them?

# After You Read

## A. Organizing Ideas

**What can you do with a simple machine?** Complete the web below. In each oval, name a simple machine and tell how it makes work easier. Refer to the article to find the information. You can also write new ideas of your own. The first oval has been done for you.

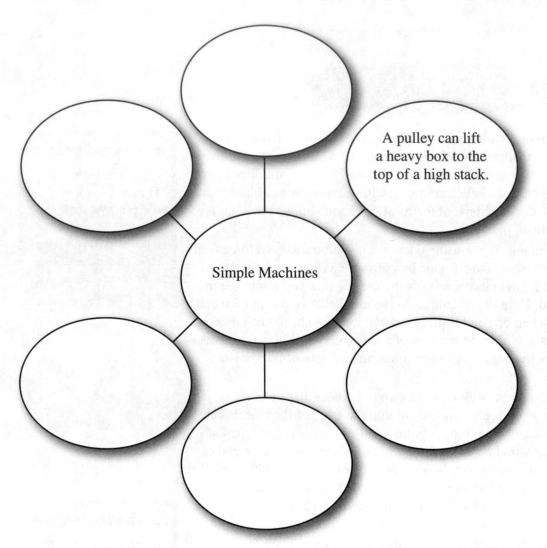

Simple Machines

A pulley can lift a heavy box to the top of a high stack.

Was it difficult to think of ways to use the simple machines? Why? Write two or more sentences explaining your answer. Did you find the web helpful for organizing what you learned from the article? How?

_____

_____

_____

_____

_____

## B. Comprehension Skills

**Tip!** **Think about how to find answers.** Look back at what you read. The words you need to complete each item are usually contained in a single sentence of the article.

Mark box **a, b,** or **c** with an **X** before the choice that best completes each sentence.

### Recalling Facts

1. A lever is
   - ☐ **a.** a simple machine.
   - ☐ **b.** a compound machine.
   - ☐ **c.** an inclined plane.

2. A seesaw is a
   - ☐ **a.** load.
   - ☐ **b.** pulley.
   - ☐ **c.** lever.

3. A pulley has
   - ☐ **a.** an inclined plane on a fulcrum.
   - ☐ **b.** a wheel that turns on an axle.
   - ☐ **c.** a lever on a rope.

4. A ramp is
   - ☐ **a.** an inclined plane.
   - ☐ **b.** a fulcrum.
   - ☐ **c.** a lever.

5. A road going up a hill is
   - ☐ **a.** a lever.
   - ☐ **b.** an inclined plane.
   - ☐ **c.** a pulley.

### Understanding Ideas

1. From the article, you can conclude that simple machines
   - ☐ **a.** are made up of many parts.
   - ☐ **b.** make daily activities easier.
   - ☐ **c.** require only a small amount of electricity.

2. To move a big rock, you would probably use
   - ☐ **a.** an inclined plane.
   - ☐ **b.** a lever.
   - ☐ **c.** a pulley.

3. By placing a wide board over a flight of stairs, you can create a
   - ☐ **a.** ramp.
   - ☐ **b.** pulley.
   - ☐ **c.** lever.

4. From the article, you can conclude that simple machines are
   - ☐ **a.** hard to use.
   - ☐ **b.** hard to find.
   - ☐ **c.** all around us.

5. You can also conclude that a crowbar is a
   - ☐ **a.** simple machine.
   - ☐ **b.** power tool.
   - ☐ **c.** fulcrum.

## C. Reading Skills

### 1. Recognizing Words in Context

Find the word *force* in the article. One definition below is closest to the meaning of that word. One definition has the opposite or nearly the opposite meaning. The remaining definition has a meaning that has nothing to do with the other two words. Label the definitions **C** for *closest,* **O** for *opposite* or *nearly opposite,* and **U** for *unrelated.*

_____ **a.** power

_____ **b.** weakness

_____ **c.** need

### 2. Distinguishing Fact from Opinion

Two of the statements below present *facts,* which can be proved. The other statement is an *opinion,* which expresses someone's thoughts or beliefs. Label the statements **F** for *fact* and **O** for *opinion.*

_____ **a.** A fulcrum is a point that stays still.

_____ **b.** Pulleys are easier to use than levers.

_____ **c.** A simple machine has very few parts.

### 3. Making Correct Inferences

Two of the statements below are correct *inferences,* or reasonable guesses, that are based on information in the article. The other statement is an incorrect inference. Label the statements **C** for *correct* inference and **I** for *incorrect* inference.

_____ **a.** Simple machines are useful tools.

_____ **b.** Carrying a load straight up is easier than pushing it up a ramp.

_____ **c.** A seesaw is a common simple machine.

### 4. Understanding Main Ideas

One of the statements below expresses the main idea of the article. Another statement is too general, or too broad. The other explains only part of the article; it is too narrow. Label the statements **M** for *main idea,* **B** for *too broad,* and **N** for *too narrow.*

_____ **a.** Simple machines help us do work.

_____ **b.** One kind of lever is a crowbar.

_____ **c.** Machines do work.

### 5. Responding to the Article

Complete the following sentence in your own words:

Before reading "Simple Machines," I already knew

_____

_____

## D. Expanding Vocabulary

### Content-Area Words

Read each item carefully. Write on the line the word or phrase that best completes each sentence.

1. We noticed a _____ cut into the edge of the pulley.

   circle          slit          groove

2. The men moved the boxes up the _____ into the warehouse.

   ramp          lever          pulley

3. When the fulcrum is the middle of a lever, applying _____ on one end raises the other.

   pulley          ramp          force

4. A machine is something that helps us _____.

   relax          do work          earn money

5. One type of lever is a(n) _____.

   ramp          axle          crowbar


### Academic English

In the article "Simple Machines," you learned that *benefits* can be a verb meaning "is helpful to." *Benefits* can also be a noun meaning "things that are useful or helpful," as in the following sentence.

   *Calcium offers many benefits for your bones and skin.*

Complete the sentence below.

1. I see the *benefits* of studying when _____

Now use the word *benefits* in a sentence of your own.

2. _____

   _____

You also learned that *complex* means "having many related parts that work together." *Complex* can also mean "hard to solve or understand," as in the following sentence.

   *It takes more time to answer a complex math problem than a simple one.*

Complete the sentence below.

3. A *complex* math problem is _____

Now use the word *complex* in two sentences of your own.

4. _____

5. _____

**Talk It Over** Share your new sentences with a partner.

## Before You Read

 **Think about what you know.** Read the title of the lesson. Who was Benjamin Franklin? What do you know about his scientific discoveries?

## Vocabulary

The content-area and academic English words below appear in "The Discoveries of Benjamin Franklin." Read the definitions and the example sentences.

### Content-Area Words

**scientists** (sī′ən tists) experts in one of the sciences
  *Example: Scientists* in the medical sciences know a great deal about medicine and diseases.

**theory** (thē′ rē) an unproved explanation based on known facts
  *Example:* The doctor's *theory* about his patient's illness was based on what he knew about the symptoms.

**experiment** (iks per′ə mənt) an action designed to discover or inform about something or to test an idea
  *Example:* Noemi's *experiment* showed her that her cactus plant needed much less water than she realized.

**forecasts** (fôr′kasts) guesses about the future, such as weather information
  *Example:* Weather *forecasts* say that it will rain tomorrow.

**inventor** (in ven′tər) a person who creates new things to improve life, work, or safety
  *Example:* The *inventor* made a snowboard for people who cannot use their legs.

### Academic English

**similar** (sim′ə lər) like something else
  *Example:* An apple and an orange are fruits that are *similar* in size.

**design** (di zīn′) plan or make something for a purpose
  *Example:* The manufacturers *design* cars for style, service, and safety.

Answer the questions below. Circle the part of each question that is the answer. The first one has been done for you.

1. Would a *scientist* study (biology) or Spanish?
2. Can people *design* weather or houses?
3. Do you prove a *theory* by guessing at it or by testing it?
4. Do people use weather *forecasts* to prepare for weather or to prevent weather?
5. Which is more *similar* to running, jogging or walking?
6. Would you do an *experiment* to hide something or to test something?
7. Does an *inventor* create things that make life easier or that serve no purpose?

**Dictionary** Now skim the article and look for other words that are new to you. Write each new word and its definition in the Personal Dictionary.

# While You Read

**Tip!** **Think about why you read.** Benjamin Franklin liked to know how and why things happen. Do you like to know how things work? As you read, look for the things that Benjamin Franklin wanted to know more about.

THE DISCOVERIES OF
## Benjamin Franklin

1   **Scientists** ask questions. They want to know why something happens. To find out, they watch what happens and then think of an idea that explains how and why it works. This kind of idea is called a **theory.** Once a scientist has a theory, he or she performs an **experiment** to see whether the theory is correct.

5   Benjamin Franklin was a scientist who lived in the 1700s. At that time, people did not understand what lightning was. Franklin guessed that it was **similar** to electricity. He knew that electricity could make short flashes of light called sparks. If Franklin could get lightning to make sparks, he would prove that lightning and electricity were the same thing.

10  Franklin thought that he could **design** a kite to attract lightning from a cloud. He built his kite by connecting two sticks and tying a large silk scarf across them. Then he put a pointed piece of metal at the top of the kite and tied a key to the end of the kite string. When he saw a storm coming, he went out into a field where there was a small shed. He sent the kite into the air and then waited in the
15  doorway until lightning began to flash. When he touched the key with his finger, he saw a spark. Before the storm had ended, he was able to make many more sparks.

Franklin made other important scientific discoveries. Years before he flew his kite, he had guessed that it would be possible to predict the direction in which
20  storms would move. To learn more about storms, he rode his horse to chase a tornado. From what he found out, Franklin made weather **forecasts.** Because he was also a printer, he printed his forecasts so that other people could read them.

In his lifetime, Franklin sailed across the Atlantic Ocean from the United States to Europe and back eight times. While he was on the ship, he was curious about
25  ocean currents. On each trip, he took the temperature of the water. His findings helped him chart one of the ocean's most important currents, the Gulf Stream.

Like some other great scientists, Franklin was an **inventor** too. What he learned from science helped him invent things to make people's lives safer and easier, such as the lightning rod. A lightning rod can protect buildings and ships from
30  lightning damage. He also built a wood stove to heat houses. It used less wood and was safer than a fireplace.

**CONTENT CONNECTION**

Lightning rods are metal rods that attract lightning to buildings. The rods carry energy from the lightning into the ground, not into a building where it might hurt people. Have you ever seen a lightning rod?

**LANGUAGE CONNECTION**

The word *curious* means "interested in learning." Scientists are curious about how the body works, what causes weather, and how to care for the environment. What subjects make you curious?

# After You Read

## A. Organizing Ideas

**What makes Benjamin Franklin important to science history?** Complete the organizer below. First, think about the main idea of the article. Then list in the boxes facts from the article that support the main idea. Write down your facts in complete sentences. The first box has been done for you.

| Benjamin Franklin was a scientist who made important discoveries and invented useful things. |
| --- |
| |
| |
| |
| |

Do you think that Benjamin Franklin's inventions are still important today? Write two or more sentences that explain your answer. How did the organizer help you reach this conclusion?

_____

_____

_____

_____

_____

_____

## B. Comprehension Skills

**Tip!** **Think about how to find answers.** Read each item carefully. Underline the words that will help you figure out how to complete each item.

Mark box **a, b,** or **c** with an **X** before the choice that best completes each sentence.

### Recalling Facts

1. A scientist's idea of how something works is called
   - ☐ **a.** an experiment.
   - ☐ **b.** a spark.
   - ☐ **c.** a theory.

2. Benjamin Franklin lived in the
   - ☐ **a.** 1700s.
   - ☐ **b.** 1600s.
   - ☐ **c.** 1800s.

3. Franklin tied the end of his kite string to a
   - ☐ **a.** key.
   - ☐ **b.** shed.
   - ☐ **c.** lightning rod.

4. Franklin put a pointed piece of metal on top of his
   - ☐ **a.** shed.
   - ☐ **b.** ship.
   - ☐ **c.** kite.

5. Franklin invented
   - ☐ **a.** keys.
   - ☐ **b.** kites.
   - ☐ **c.** lightning rods.

### Understanding Ideas

1. Scientists do experiments to
   - ☐ **a.** ask questions.
   - ☐ **b.** learn whether a theory is correct.
   - ☐ **c.** change the weather.

2. Benjamin Franklin proved that
   - ☐ **a.** lightning and electricity are different.
   - ☐ **b.** lightning is electricity.
   - ☐ **c.** kites can fly.

3. The article suggests that Franklin thought that a kite with metal attached to it could
   - ☐ **a.** attract lightning.
   - ☐ **b.** show when a storm would occur.
   - ☐ **c.** measure the distance to the clouds.

4. From the article, you can conclude that Franklin was a true scientist because he
   - ☐ **a.** was an inventor.
   - ☐ **b.** made some important scientific discoveries.
   - ☐ **c.** published his own weather forecasts.

5. To find out how wood floats, you might first
   - ☐ **a.** think of a theory.
   - ☐ **b.** take the temperature of the water.
   - ☐ **c.** test a theory about how plastic floats.

## C. Reading Strategies

### 1. Recognizing Words in Context

Find the word *curious* in the article. One definition below is closest to the meaning of that word. One definition has the opposite or nearly the opposite meaning. The remaining definition has a meaning that has nothing to do with the other two words. Label the definitions **C** for *closest,* **O** for *opposite* or *nearly opposite,* and **U** for *unrelated.*

_____ **a.** uninterested

_____ **b.** interested

_____ **c.** disgusted

### 2. Distinguishing Fact from Opinion

Two of the statements below present *facts,* which can be proved. The other statement is an *opinion,* which expresses someone's thoughts or beliefs. Label the statements **F** for *fact* and **O** for *opinion.*

_____ **a.** Franklin thought that lightning was electricity.

_____ **b.** Franklin charted the Gulf Stream current.

_____ **c.** The 1700s were difficult years in America.

### 3. Making Correct Inferences

Two of the statements below are correct *inferences,* or reasonable guesses, that are based on information in the article. The other statement is an incorrect inference. Label the statements **C** for *correct* inference and **I** for *incorrect* inference.

_____ **a.** Franklin predicted the weather from what he knew about storms.

_____ **b.** Franklin could publish information about his experiments.

_____ **c.** Franklin invented dangerous things.

### 4. Understanding Main Ideas

One of the statements below expresses the main idea of the article. Another statement is too general, or too broad. The other explains only part of the article; it is too narrow. Label the statements **M** for *main idea,* **B** for *too broad,* and **N** for *too narrow.*

_____ **a.** Scientists ask questions, form hypotheses, and do experiments.

_____ **b.** Benjamin Franklin was a scientist.

_____ **c.** Benjamin Franklin made several important scientific discoveries.

### 5. Responding to the Article

Complete the following sentence in your own words:

What I found most interesting in "The Discoveries of Benjamin Franklin" was

_____

_____

## D. Expanding Vocabulary

### Content-Area Words

Complete each analogy with a word from the box. Write in the missing word.

| scientists | theory | experiments | forecasts | inventor |

**1.** movies : actor :: _____ : scientist

**2.** news : reporter :: _____ : meteorologist

**3.** artist : picture :: _____ : invention

**4.** teachers : school :: _____ : laboratory

**5.** academy : school :: _____ : idea

### Academic English

In the article "The Discoveries of Benjamin Franklin," you learned that *similar* means "like something else." *Similar* can be used to compare things in science, such as lightning and electricity. *Similar* can also be used to compare the meanings of words, as in the following sentence.

> *The words* afraid *and* scared *have similar meanings; they both mean "fearful" or "frightened."*

Complete the sentence below.

**1.** Many words have meanings that are *similar* to the word *happy*, such as _____

Now use the word *similar* in a sentence of your own.

**2.** _____

You also learned that *design* is a verb meaning "plan or make something for a purpose." *Design* can also be a noun meaning "something planned or made for a purpose," as in the following sentence.

> *My science project is a new design for an electric car.*

Complete the sentence below.

**3.** I wish an inventor would make a *design* for a machine that would _____

Now use the word *design* in two sentences of your own.

**4.** _____

**5.** _____

Share your new sentences with a partner.

# Before You Read

 **Think about what you know.** Read the title and the first sentence of the article on the opposite page. What things have you have heard about sharks?

## Vocabulary

The content-area and academic English words below appear in "The Truth About Sharks." Read the definitions and the example sentences.

### Content-Area Words

**mammals** (mam′əlz) warm-blooded animals that give birth to live young and produce milk
*Example:* Because they lay eggs, fish are not *mammals*.

**primitive** (prim′ə tiv) crude or simple, not fancy
*Example:* A hut is a *primitive* home.

**currents** (kur′ənts) streams of air, water, or electricity that flow in a certain direction
*Example:* *Currents* of air can cool off a hot room.

**intensify** (in ten′sə fī) make stronger
*Example:* Salt can *intensify* the flavor of food.

**scavengers** (skav′in jərz) animals that feed on dead or decaying plants or animals
*Example:* Vultures are *scavengers* that feed on animals that are already dead.

### Academic English

**analyzed** (a′nə līzd′) studied (something) carefully to learn how it works
*Example:* The student *analyzed* the question before attempting to answer it.

**identify** (ī den′tə fī′) recognize or discover what something is
*Example:* You may be able to *identify* a friend from a distance by his walk.

Answer the questions below. Circle the part of each question that is the answer. The first one has been done for you.

1. Would a *mammal* lay eggs or have young without shells?
2. Would a communication system that is *primitive* be easy or difficult to use?
3. To *intensify* your workload, would you work more or fewer hours?
4. If you wanted *currents* of air in the room, would you open the window or close it?
5. Would a *scavenger* be more likely to eat meat or plants?
6. Would the police use a fingerprint or a bus schedule to *identify* a criminal?
7. If you *analyzed* a problem, would you be solving it or not thinking about it?

**Dictionary** Now skim the article and look for other words that are new to you. Write each new word and its definition in the Personal Dictionary.

# While You Read

**Tip!** **Think about why you read.** Think about a myth. Why is a myth called a myth? Then read the article. As you read, look for the main idea about sharks.

## THE TRUTH ABOUT SHARKS

1  There are many myths, or false ideas, about sharks. One idea is that sharks like to eat people. Although some sharks can eat people, we are not really on their menu. Sharks usually eat fish or sea mammals such as seals, especially if the fish or **mammals** are weak or dead. Many sharks have rows of sharp teeth. When teeth
5  are lost, other teeth move in to replace them.

The whale shark—which is not a whale—is Earth's biggest fish. Whales are bigger than sharks, but they are mammals, not fish. The great white shark is perhaps the most dangerous to people. Great whites are large sharks that are known to attack people. Such attacks are rare, though. It is believed that they take
10  place when a shark mistakes a person for something else.

Because sharks have been on Earth for thousands of years, they are thought to be **primitive,** simple animals. This is another myth. Sharks are really very complex creatures. They have a powerful sense of smell and sharp hearing. Some have organs on their long noses, or snouts, that pick up electric **currents** made by
15  the muscles of swimming fish. Sharks have large brains, and they learn quickly. They have memory and can be trained.

Another myth about sharks is that they do not see well. Sharks actually have good vision, especially in dim light. They have a layer of cells at the back of the eye that works like a mirror to **intensify** the light.

20  One myth created by movies is that the fin on a shark's back rises above the water when it is getting ready to attack. The truth is that a shark often attacks from below, without showing its fin above the surface.

Many people believe that sharks are dangerous. Some of these people think it would be better if there were no sharks. But sharks are useful to humans. They are
25  **scavengers** that clean up garbage from ships and waste from the ocean. They help other species of sea animals stay strong by eating animals that are sick or weak.

Much of what we know about sharks comes from the scientists who have **analyzed** them. The scientist Eugenie Clark has made many dives to study sharks. She has also studied sharks in her lab. For example, she trained them to press a
30  target to get food and learned how sharks can **identify** color and shape. Because of her work with sharks, some people call Clark the Shark Lady.

**LANGUAGE CONNECTION**

What makes the phrase *on their menu* seem funny in a science article?

**CONTENT CONNECTION**

The shark is near the top of the *food chain*, a ranking of creatures according to whether they eat or are eaten by others. Why do you think the shark's position is so high on this chain?

# After You Read

## A. Organizing Ideas

**What are the most common myths about sharks?** Complete the chart below by supplying information from the article that tells what is—and is not—true about this amazing creature. In the left column, write down myths, or statements that are not true. In the right column, write down facts, or statements that are true, that show why the myths are untrue. The first one has been done for you.

| Myths About Sharks | Facts About Sharks |
|---|---|
| People are the favorite food of sharks. | Sharks usually eat fish or sea mammals. |
| The whale is Earth's biggest fish. | |
| | Sharks are complex creatures with powerful senses (smell, hearing, and sight). |
| A shark preparing to attack lifts its back fin above water level. | |
| | Sharks have good vision, especially in dim light. |
| Sharks are mean; it would be better if there were no sharks. | |

What conclusion did you reach after completing this chart? Write one or two sentences about your conclusion. Then explain how this chart helped you reach this conclusion.

_____

_____

_____

_____

## B. Comprehension Skills

**Tip!** **Think about how to find answers.** Look back at what you read. The information is in the text, but you may have to look in several sentences to find it.

Mark box **a, b,** or **c** with an **X** before the choice that best completes each sentence.

### Recalling Facts

1. One myth about sharks is that they
   - ☐ **a.** have sharp hearing.
   - ☐ **b.** rarely attack human beings.
   - ☐ **c.** do not see well from a distance.

2. A shark
   - ☐ **a.** does not see very well.
   - ☐ **b.** can see well in dim light.
   - ☐ **c.** sees well only from close up.

3. Some sharks have organs on their faces that
   - ☐ **a.** pick up electric currents.
   - ☐ **b.** let them grow new teeth.
   - ☐ **c.** help them see in dim light.

4. Earth's biggest fish is the
   - ☐ **a.** whale shark.
   - ☐ **b.** blue whale.
   - ☐ **c.** great white shark.

5. The scientist Eugenie Clark trained sharks to
   - ☐ **a.** eat garbage from ships.
   - ☐ **b.** press a target to get food.
   - ☐ **c.** raise and lower their back fins.

### Understanding Ideas

1. From the article, you can conclude that sharks
   - ☐ **a.** are a threat to ships.
   - ☐ **b.** play a positive role in nature.
   - ☐ **c.** are primitive, simple animals.

2. Sharks are most likely to eat
   - ☐ **a.** people.
   - ☐ **b.** other fish.
   - ☐ **c.** squid.

3. Sharks can be trained because they
   - ☐ **a.** have sharp hearing.
   - ☐ **b.** are scavengers.
   - ☐ **c.** have memory.

4. It is likely that Eugenie Clark
   - ☐ **a.** is an experienced diver.
   - ☐ **b.** is afraid of sharks.
   - ☐ **c.** does not like fish.

5. Most of what we think we know about sharks we
   - ☐ **a.** learned from history books.
   - ☐ **b.** learn from the movies.
   - ☐ **c.** learn from scientists.

## C. Reading Strategies

### 1. Recognizing Words in Context

Find the word *dim* in the article. One definition below is closest to the meaning of that word. One definition has the opposite or nearly the opposite meaning. The remaining definition has a meaning that has nothing to do with the other two words. Label the definitions **C** for *closest*, **O** for *opposite* or *nearly opposite*, and **U** for *unrelated*.

_____ **a.** bright

_____ **b.** dark

_____ **c.** ugly

### 2. Distinguishing Fact from Opinion

Two of the statements below present *facts*, which can be proved. The other statement is an *opinion*, which expresses someone's thoughts or beliefs. Label the statements **F** for *fact* and **O** for *opinion*.

_____ **a.** Sharks are more dangerous than tigers.

_____ **b.** Sharks can see well in dim light.

_____ **c.** Sharks are helpful in the ocean.

### 3. Making Correct Inferences

Two of the statements below are correct *inferences*, or reasonable guesses, that are based on information in the article. The other statement is an incorrect inference. Label the statements **C** for *correct* inference and **I** for *incorrect* inference.

_____ **a.** Shark attacks occur often.

_____ **b.** Eugenie Clark has learned a lot about sharks.

_____ **c.** The ocean might get dirty if sharks did not exist.

### 4. Understanding Main Ideas

One of the statements below expresses the main idea of the article. Another statement is too general, or too broad. The other explains only part of the article; it is too narrow. Label the statements **M** for *main idea*, **B** for *too broad*, and **N** for *too narrow*.

_____ **a.** Sharks eat fish and sea mammals such as seals.

_____ **b.** Sharks are smart, helpful fish that most people do not know much about.

_____ **c.** Sharks live in the ocean.

### 5. Responding to the Article

Complete the following sentence in your own words:

What I found most interesting in "The Truth About Sharks" was

_____

_____

_____

_____

## D. Expanding Vocabulary

### Content-Area Words

Complete each sentence with a word from the box. Write the missing word on the line.

| mammals | primitive | currents | intensify | scavengers |

**1.** A shack could be called a _____ house.

**2.** Vultures are _____ because they eat animals that have died.

**3.** Some water _____ in the Pacific Ocean warm the shoreline that they pass.

**4.** The hot rays of the sun _____ as spring turns to summer.

**5.** Some _____ are often mistaken for fish.

### Academic English

In the article "The Truth About Sharks," you learned that *analyzed* means "studied (something) carefully to learn how it works." In the article, *analyzed* describes how scientists study sharks. *Analyzed* can also apply to other kinds of study, as in the following sentence.

> *People have analyzed history so that we can learn from our mistakes.*

Complete the sentence below.

**1.** As students *analyze* a mathematics problem, they_____

Now use the word *analyzed* in a sentence of your own.

**2.** _____

_____

You also learned that *identify* means "recognize or discover what something is." *Identify* can also mean "think of as related," as in the following sentence.

> *People usually identify actors with the movies they were in.*

Complete the sentence below.

**3.** I *identify* the color red with _____

Now use the word *identify* in two sentences of your own.

**4.** _____

**5.** _____

**Talk It Over** Share your new sentences with a partner.

# Before You Read

**Tip!** **Think about what you know.** Skim the article on the opposite page. Have you ever noticed the different kinds of clouds in the sky?

## Vocabulary

The content-area and academic English words below appear in "Types of Clouds." Read the definitions and the example sentences.

### Content-Area Words

**vertically** (vur′ti kəl ē) upright; the opposite of *horizontally*
> *Example:* You hold your body *vertically* when you are standing.

**cirrus** (sir′əs) describing thin white clouds made of ice crystals found high above Earth
> *Example:* *Cirrus* clouds appear in thin layers high in the sky.

**altostratus** (al′tō strat′əs) describing a light gray layer of clouds found in the middle of the atmosphere
> *Example:* Clouds that look gray are probably *altostratus* clouds.

**fog** (fôg) small water droplets that hang in the air close to Earth's surface, making the air look smoky
> *Example:* The thick *fog* in the air made it difficult to see the road ahead.

**cumulonimbus** (kū′myə lō nim′bəs) describing cumulus clouds that rise upward like a tower and often bring thunderstorms
> *Example:* Large, dark *cumulonimbus* clouds are a sign that a storm is coming.

### Academic English

**vary** (vār′ē) to have different kinds or types
> *Example:* Most people *vary* their meals, but I enjoy eating the same things often.

**located** (lō′kāt əd) settled in a certain place
> *Example:* The Rocky Mountains are *located* in the western United States.

Answer the questions below about the content-area and academic English words. Write your answers in the spaces provided. The first one has been done for you.

1. What word goes with *thick air that appears smoky?* _____fog_____
2. What word goes with *clouds that look like a tower?* _____
3. What word goes with *standing straight up?* _____
4. What word goes with *do something different each day?* _____
5. What word goes with *clouds made of ice crystals?* _____
6. What word goes with *in the place where something is settled?* _____
7. What word goes with *gray clouds?* _____

 **Dictionary** Now skim the article and look for other words that are new to you. Write each new word and its definition in the Personal Dictionary.

# While You Read

**Tip!** **Think about why you read.** Clouds come in many types and shapes. Do you know what makes types of clouds different from one another? As you read, try to find the answer.

## Types of Clouds

1 Have you ever watched clouds on a summer day? Cloud shapes **vary.** One cloud may look like a woolly sheep, and another one may remind you of a dog's tail. Some clouds may look like ocean waves or mountains. You will notice that there seem to be many different kinds of clouds. Some are high and thin,
5 some are white and fluffy, and others seem dark and heavy.

Actually, there are four kinds of clouds. They are high clouds, middle clouds, low clouds, and clouds that grow **vertically.** The clouds in these groups are named for the way they look.

**Cirrus** clouds are high clouds that are **located** more than 5 kilometers (3 miles)
10 above Earth. The air that high in the sky is very cold. Cirrus clouds are made of ice crystals so light that the wind blows them into thin layers. The word *cirrus* means "curl of hair." Some high clouds that look like layers or sheets are called cirrostratus clouds. The word *stratus* means "layer." There are other high clouds that look like clumps of cotton. These are the cirrocumulus clouds. *Cumulus*
15 means "heap."

About 3 to 6.5 kilometers (2 to 4 miles) above Earth are the middle clouds, but they can be found low in the sky too. **Altostratus** clouds are light gray and can form a layer that looks like a blanket. Altocumulus clouds are very fluffy. They often are scattered across the sky.

20 Low clouds are no higher up than about 1.6 kilometers (1 mile) above Earth. Two kinds of clouds are often found here. Stratocumulus clouds are both light and dark. They are made up of piles of fluffy clouds. Stratus clouds are very low clouds that spread out in a gray layer. They often give off moisture in the form of drizzle. Sometimes these clouds form very close to the ground. Then they are
25 called **fog.** Another cloud that sometimes is found in the low area (but may also be found in the middle area) is the nimbostratus cloud. *Nimbo* comes from the word *nimbus*, which means "vapor" or "rain." These clouds form a dark gray layer. Rain and snow fall from nimbostratus clouds.

The fourth group of clouds grows vertically. These clouds start near the ground
30 but rise to a great height. Cumulus clouds can pile up on top of one another. When they pile up high, they are called **cumulonimbus** clouds. These cloud towers can rise as high as 18 kilometers (11 miles)! Cumulonimbus clouds are also known as thunderheads because they bring thunderstorms.

**CONTENT CONNECTION**

The main idea of this paragraph does not appear in the first sentence. Which sentence contains the main idea? Can you see clouds outside today? What kind?

**LANGUAGE CONNECTION**

*Drizzle* is a noun that means "a light rain." *Drizzle* can also be a verb meaning "to drop liquid lightly." You can drizzle chocolate syrup on ice cream. What else can you drizzle?

# After You Read

## A. Organizing Ideas

**Where in the sky can you see different types of clouds?** Complete the chart. Write the cloud types that match the location in each box. Write both the name of the cloud and a short description. One item in each box in the left column has been done for you.

| Position in the Sky | Vertical Arrangement |
|---|---|
| **High**<br>Cirrus clouds—high clouds made of ice crystals | Cumulus clouds—thick, puffy clouds |
| **Middle**<br>Altocumulus—fluffy clouds that are often scattered across the sky | |
| **Low**<br>Stratocumulus clouds—light and dark clouds made up of piles of fluffy clouds | |

Did you already know some of the cloud types? List the names of the clouds described in the article that were new to you. Tell how you will remember and recognize them. How will preparing this chart help you?

_____

_____

_____

_____

_____

## B. Comprehension Skills

**Tip!** **Think about how to find answers.** Look back at different parts of the text. What facts help you figure out how to complete each item?

Mark box **a**, **b**, or **c** with an **X** before the choice that best completes each sentence.

### Recalling Facts

1. Middle clouds are
   - ☐ **a.** at least 13 kilometers above Earth.
   - ☐ **b.** about 3 to 6.5 kilometers above Earth.
   - ☐ **c.** 1.6 kilometers above Earth.

2. Cirrus clouds are
   - ☐ **a.** high clouds.
   - ☐ **b.** clouds that grow vertically.
   - ☐ **c.** middle clouds.

3. Altostratus clouds are
   - ☐ **a.** clouds that grow vertically.
   - ☐ **b.** middle clouds.
   - ☐ **c.** fog.

4. Cumulonimbus clouds are also called
   - ☐ **a.** nimbostratus.
   - ☐ **b.** high clouds.
   - ☐ **c.** thunderheads.

5. *Cirrus* means
   - ☐ **a.** "curl of hair."
   - ☐ **b.** "heap."
   - ☐ **c.** "layer."

### Understanding Ideas

1. From the article, you can conclude that a cirrus cloud is a
   - ☐ **a.** cold cloud.
   - ☐ **b.** low cloud.
   - ☐ **c.** warm cloud.

2. The article suggests that fog is
   - ☐ **a.** hot.
   - ☐ **b.** a cirrus cloud.
   - ☐ **c.** moist.

3. From the article, you can conclude that clouds that form heaps can be
   - ☐ **a.** only low clouds.
   - ☐ **b.** only high clouds.
   - ☐ **c.** high, middle, and low clouds.

4. You can also conclude that clouds that grow vertically are
   - ☐ **a.** flat.
   - ☐ **b.** tall.
   - ☐ **c.** low.

5. You are most likely to see a cumulonimbus cloud
   - ☐ **a.** just before a storm.
   - ☐ **b.** in a clear sky.
   - ☐ **c.** lying near the ground.

## C. Reading Strategies

### 1. Recognizing Words in Context

Find the word *thin* in the article. One definition below is closest to the meaning of that word. One definition has the opposite or nearly the opposite meaning. The remaining definition has a meaning that has nothing to do with the other two words. Label the definitions **C** for *closest*, **O** for *opposite* or *nearly opposite*, and **U** for *unrelated*.

_____ **a.** wide

_____ **b.** pale

_____ **c.** narrow

### 2. Distinguishing Fact from Opinion

Two of the statements below present *facts*, which can be proved. The other statement is an *opinion*, which expresses someone's thoughts or beliefs. Label the statements **F** for *fact* and **O** for *opinion*.

_____ **a.** Altostratus clouds are usually shaped like animals.

_____ **b.** Clouds are named for how they look.

_____ **c.** Stratus clouds are very low clouds.

### 3. Making Correct Inferences

Two of the statements below are correct *inferences*, or reasonable guesses, that are based on information in the article. The other statement is an incorrect inference. Label the statements **C** for *correct* inference and **I** for *incorrect* inference.

_____ **a.** Airplanes cannot fly through cumulus clouds.

_____ **b.** Clouds that seem to be "heaped" on top of one another are probably cumulonimbus clouds.

_____ **c.** You may need your boots if you see nimbostratus clouds.

### 4. Understanding Main Ideas

One of the statements below expresses the main idea of the article. Another statement is too general, or too broad. The other explains only part of the article; it is too narrow. Label the statements **M** for *main idea*, **B** for *too broad*, and **N** for *too narrow*.

_____ **a.** Cumulonimbus clouds are also known as thunderheads.

_____ **b.** Clouds are a wonder of nature.

_____ **c.** There are four types of clouds, and they are named for the way they look.

### 5. Responding to the Article

Complete the following sentence in your own words:

From reading "Types of Clouds," I have learned

_____

_____

## D. Expanding Vocabulary

### Content-Area Words

Read each item carefully.

Mark box **a, b,** or **c** with an **X** before the choice that best completes the sentence.

1. The pilots could not see through the fog
   - ☐ **a.** curls.
   - ☐ **b.** cirrus.
   - ☐ **c.** clouds.

2. Fluffy altostratus clouds can look like a
   - ☐ **a.** sheep.
   - ☐ **b.** blanket.
   - ☐ **c.** pile.

3. Cumulus clouds that pile up are called
   - ☐ **a.** cumulonimbus clouds.
   - ☐ **b.** cirrus clouds.
   - ☐ **c.** stratus clouds.

4. Cirrus clouds get their shape from ice
   - ☐ **a.** cubes.
   - ☐ **b.** crystals.
   - ☐ **c.** flakes.

5. Because cumulonimbus clouds bring storms, we often call them
   - ☐ **a.** layers.
   - ☐ **b.** dangerous.
   - ☐ **c.** thunderheads.

### Academic English

In the article "Types of Clouds," you learned that *vary* means "to have different kinds or types." *Vary* can also mean "to change types," as in the following sentence.

*You should vary what you eat, because you need different foods to be healthy.*

Complete the sentence below.

**1.** I try to *vary* the kinds of exercise I do to _____

Now use the word *vary* in a sentence of your own.

**2.** _____

You also learned that *located* can be a predicate adjective meaning "settled in a certain place." *Located* can also be a verb meaning "found the place of something," as in the following sentence.

*I located the address by following your directions.*

Complete the sentence below.

**3.** You may have *located* other continents or countries by looking at a _____

Now use the word *located* in two sentences of your own.

**4.** _____

**5.** _____

**Talk It Over** Share your new sentences with a partner.

## Writing a Brochure

Read the brochure. Then complete the sentences. Use words from the Word Bank.

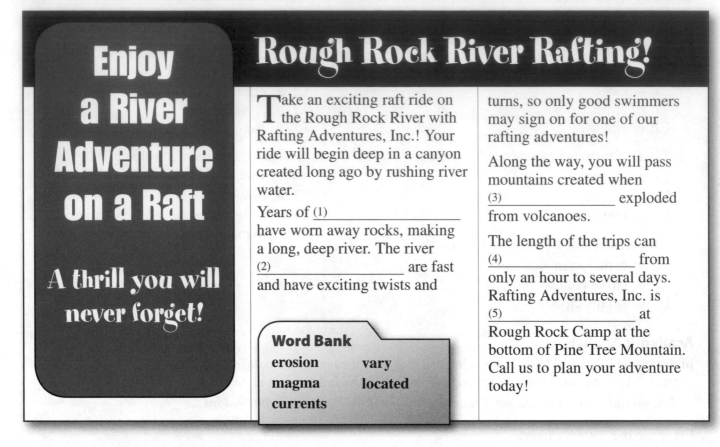

**Enjoy a River Adventure on a Raft**

*A thrill you will never forget!*

### Rough Rock River Rafting!

Take an exciting raft ride on the Rough Rock River with Rafting Adventures, Inc.! Your ride will begin deep in a canyon created long ago by rushing river water.

Years of (1) _____ have worn away rocks, making a long, deep river. The river (2) _____ are fast and have exciting twists and turns, so only good swimmers may sign on for one of our rafting adventures!

Along the way, you will pass mountains created when (3) _____ exploded from volcanoes.

The length of the trips can (4) _____ from only an hour to several days. Rafting Adventures, Inc. is (5) _____ at Rough Rock Camp at the bottom of Pine Tree Mountain. Call us to plan your adventure today!

**Word Bank**

erosion          vary
magma          located
currents

## Reading a Newspaper Article

Read the article. Circle the word in parentheses that completes each sentence.

## Daily News • Science

# Town Prepares for Possible Eruption
### by Carmen Marquez

The town of Sunny Valley is preparing! Big Cloud Mountain may erupt at any time. Big Cloud is one of two (**lithospheres, volcanoes**) in our state. It has been still and quiet now for more than 85 years. However, some experts are making (**forecasts, sections**) that it could erupt again. The last eruption sent hot lava and gases hundreds of feet into the air. (**Inventors, Scientists**) who have been studying Big Cloud are worried. If an eruption (**occurs, benefits**) again, it could be even greater than before.

Big Cloud is a popular place for tourists at this time of year. The mountain rises more than 10,000 feet (**similar, vertically**) into the air. Many people like to hike and picnic along its trails. Experts are warning those who plan to visit Sunny Valley to listen to the news before they go there for the vacation of their lives.

**Making Connections**

Work with a partner. Talk about what the words mean. How can you use the words to talk about a trip into outer space? List your ideas in the space below.

| machine | benefits | complex | theory | experiment |
|---------|----------|---------|--------|------------|
| design | inventor | analyzed | identify | cirrus |

Use all of the words above in complete sentences of your own. Each sentence may include one or more of the words. To help you start writing, look at the ideas you wrote about. After you write your sentences, read them over. If you find a mistake, correct it.

_____

_____

_____

_____

_____

_____

_____

_____

## Before You Read

 **Think about what you know.** Read the title and the first sentence of the article on the opposite page. What foods do you eat to stay healthy?

### Vocabulary

The content-area and academic English words below appear in "A Key to Good Health." Read the definitions and the example sentences.

**Content-Area Words**

**fiber** (fī′bər) plant material that cannot be digested by the body and so helps push waste from the body during digestion
> *Example:* Broccoli is good for you because the *fiber* in it helps you process the food.

**phytochemicals** (fī′tō kem′i kəls) substances found in plants that help the body stay healthy
> *Example:* The vitamin C in this orange is a *phytochemical* that helps me stay healthy.

**disease** (di zēz′) an infection or illness caused by bacteria, viruses, or the body's failure to work properly
> *Example:* A cold is a common *disease*.

**vitamins** (vī′tə mins) natural substances in food that are necessary to keep the body healthy
> *Example:* He is sick because he did not eat foods that were full of *vitamins*.

**nutrients** (noo′trē ənts) nutritious substances, such as minerals and vitamins, that help the body function
> *Example:* Our bodies get many *nutrients* from a variety of foods.

**Academic English**

**consume** (kən soom′) to eat
> *Example:* I found it impossible to *consume* so much food.

**alternative** (ôl tur′nə tiv) a possible choice between items
> *Example:* If I cannot play football, one *alternative* will be to play basketball.

Answer the questions below about the content-area and academic English words. Write your answers in the space provided. The first one has been done for you.

1. What word goes with *natural substance found in food?* __vitamins__
2. What word goes with *pushing waste from the body?* _____
3. What word goes with *minerals and vitamins?* _____
4. What word goes with *plant substances?* _____
5. What word goes with *bacteria or viruses?* _____
6. What word goes with *eating?* _____
7. What word goes with *making a choice?* _____

**Dictionary** Now skim the article and look for other words that are new to you. Write each new word and its definition in the Personal Dictionary.

# While You Read

**Tip!** **Think about why you read.** A serving is the amount of food someone eats at one time. How many servings of vegetables and fruits do you eat each day? As you read, find out how many servings you should eat to stay healthy.

## A Key to Good Health

1   Each of us should eat five to nine servings of fruits and vegetables a day. In fact, one-third of all the things we eat should be fruits and vegetables. This may seem like a lot. However, if you can do it, your body will thank you.

    Fruits and vegetables are plants. When we **consume** them, we get the energy
5   that the plants get from the sun. Plants contain water, which satisfies thirst. They have **fiber,** which can help rid our bodies of harmful waste. Eating raw vegetables can also help keep our teeth clean and strong.

    Plant foods are high in **phytochemicals.** (*Phyto* means "plant.") These plant chemicals work in many ways to help us stay healthy. They fight **disease** and
10  make our bodies work better. Plants that have bright colors—such as red, green, and yellow—contain the most phytochemicals. Most orange vegetables contain beta carotene. This substance allows our bodies to produce vitamin A. We need vitamin A to help us see and to keep our skin healthy. Foods such as oranges, melons, and broccoli are full of vitamin C. Vitamin C helps keep body tissues
15  strong and healthy. Why not just take **vitamins** in a pill? Most vitamin pills do not have as many kinds of vitamins as plants do. Also, the vitamins in plants are easier for our bodies to use than the vitamins in pills are.

    Unfortunately, most young people eat only one or two servings of fruits and vegetables a day. It is not hard to add fruits and vegetables to your diet. Put fruit
20  on cereal for breakfast. Munch raw vegetables at lunch as an **alternative** to chips. A glass of real fruit juice instead of a soda is a healthful choice. Many fruits and vegetables make easy snacks. Eat a banana after school. Have a handful of grapes or an apple while you do your homework. Other ways to work in the five to nine daily servings of fruits and vegetables you need include having a salad with
25  dinner and a slice of melon for dessert.

    A fruit or vegetable smoothie is a tasty dessert. To make a smoothie, cut up bananas, strawberries, or peaches, or combine them. Then put them into a blender, along with a small amount of juice, milk, or yogurt. Frozen yogurt can be added to make the smoothie thicker. Both fruits and vegetables can be used
30  to make smoothies for desserts. Smoothies can provide important **nutrients** and taste delicious.

**LANGUAGE CONNECTION**

*Phyto* is a prefix, a word part that comes at the beginning of a word. Can you think of any words that begin with the prefix *non–*?

**CONTENT CONNECTION**

You have learned that it is important to eat nutritious foods. What other things do you do to keep yourself healthy?

# After You Read

## A. Organizing Ideas

**How do different foods help our bodies?** Complete the chart below by thinking about how plants help our bodies function. In the left column, list three substances found in plants. In the right column, write down ways each substance helps the body. Refer to the article to help you. The first one has been done for you.

| Found in Plants | How It Helps the Body |
|---|---|
| phytochemical | fights disease |
|  |  |
|  |  |
|  |  |

How did this chart help you understand the ways plants help us stay healthy? Write two or more sentences about how eating fruits and vegetables can keep us healthy. Why would you use a chart like this again to organize information?

_____

_____

_____

_____

_____

_____

_____

## B. Comprehension Skills

**Tip!** **Think about how to find answers.** Look back at what you read. The information is in the text, but you may have to look in several sentences to find it.

Mark box **a, b,** or **c** with an **X** before the choice that best completes each sentence.

### Recalling Facts

1. Every day we should eat five to nine servings of
   ☐ **a.** fruits.
   ☐ **b.** fruits and vegetables.
   ☐ **c.** vegetables.

2. Phytochemicals
   ☐ **a.** help fight disease.
   ☐ **b.** are vitamin pills.
   ☐ **c.** are found in meat.

3. Beta carotene is found in
   ☐ **a.** fiber.
   ☐ **b.** orange vegetables.
   ☐ **c.** green vegetables.

4. Vitamins in pill form are
   ☐ **a.** harder for our bodies to use than those in plants.
   ☐ **b.** easier for our bodies to use than those in plants.
   ☐ **c.** the same as those in plants.

5. The amount of fruits and vegetables that most young people eat is
   ☐ **a.** three times as much as they need.
   ☐ **b.** twice as much as they need.
   ☐ **c.** less than half as much as they need.

### Understanding Ideas

1. To stay healthy, we should
   ☐ **a.** eat plenty of fruits and vegetables.
   ☐ **b.** eat the food that tastes best.
   ☐ **c.** avoid phytochemicals.

2. We are likely to find the most phytochemicals in
   ☐ **a.** yellow corn.
   ☐ **b.** white onions.
   ☐ **c.** green broccoli.

3. Of the following vegetables, the one that has the most beta carotene is
   ☐ **a.** a carrot.
   ☐ **b.** lettuce.
   ☐ **c.** a potato.

4. Of the following desserts, the most healthful one is
   ☐ **a.** pecan pie.
   ☐ **b.** fresh strawberries.
   ☐ **c.** premium ice cream.

5. From the article, you can conclude that
   ☐ **a.** it is important to eat a variety of fruits and vegetables.
   ☐ **b.** vegetables should always be cooked before being eaten.
   ☐ **c.** it is best to have fruit only for dessert.

## C. Reading Strategies

### 1. Recognizing Words in Context

Find the word *healthful* in the article. One definition below is closest to the meaning of that word. One definition has the opposite or nearly the opposite meaning. The remaining definition has a meaning that has nothing to do with the other two words. Label the definitions **C** for *closest,* **O** for *opposite* or *nearly opposite,* and **U** for *unrelated.*

_____ **a.** disgusting

_____ **b.** nutritious

_____ **c.** harmful

### 2. Distinguishing Fact from Opinion

Two of the statements below present *facts,* which can be proved. The other statement is an *opinion,* which expresses someone's thoughts or beliefs. Label the statements **F** for *fact* and **O** for *opinion.*

_____ **a.** Vitamin A helps our eyes and skin stay healthy.

_____ **b.** Adding raw vegetables to our diet can help us keep our teeth healthy.

_____ **c.** Vitamins found in vegetables taste bitter.

### 3. Making Correct Inferences

Two of the statements below are correct *inferences,* or reasonable guesses, that are based on information in the article. The other statement is an incorrect inference. Label the statements **C** for *correct* inference and **I** for *incorrect* inference.

_____ **a.** Many young people do not eat enough fruits or vegetables.

_____ **b.** Vitamins and other nutrients are important for good health.

_____ **c.** Soda, bananas, and grapes are healthful sources of vitamins.

### 4. Understanding Main Ideas

One of the statements below expresses the main idea of the article. Another statement is too general, or too broad. The other explains only part of the article; it is too narrow. Label the statements **M** for *main idea,* **B** for *too broad,* and **N** for *too narrow.*

_____ **a.** Fruits and vegetables contain nutrients important for health.

_____ **b.** Your body needs healthful food.

_____ **c.** Vitamin C can be found in oranges and melons.

### 5. Responding to the Article

Complete the following sentence in your own words:

Before reading "A Key to Good Health," I already knew

_____

_____

## D. Expanding Vocabulary

### Content-Area Words

Complete each sentence with a word from the box. Write the missing word on the line.

| fiber | phytochemicals | nutrients | diseases | vitamins |

1. A red, yellow, or green fruit or vegetable supplies healthful _____.

2. Foods high in _____ help remove harmful substances from our bodies.

3. Many _____ can be prevented by eating five to nine servings of fruits and vegetables each day.

4. The _____ found in plants are easier for our bodies to use than those in pills.

5. Smoothies are healthful because they are filled with _____.

### Academic English

In the article "A Key to Good Health," you learned that *consume* means "to eat." *Consume* can also mean "to destroy," as in the following sentence.

*Flames can consume a house when there is a fire.*

Complete the sentence below.

1. Rushing water can *consume* homes and cars when there is a _____

Now use the word *consume* in a sentence of your own.

2. _____

_____

You also learned that *alternative* means "a possible choice between items." *Alternative* can also mean "something other than the usual system," as in the following sentence.

*When her doctor seemed unable to help her, the woman tried alternative medicine.*

Now complete the sentence below.

3. If you don't enjoy running for exercise, try an *alternative* such as _____

Now use the word *alternative* in two sentences of your own.

4. _____

5. _____

**Talk It Over** Share your new sentences with a partner.

# Before You Read

**Tip!** **Think about what you know.** Read the title of the article. What do you think the article will be about? What do you know about ways people traveled long ago?

## Vocabulary

The content-area and academic English words below appear in "Crossing the Land with Steam Power." Read the definitions and the example sentences.

### Content-Area Words

**locomotives** (lō'kə mō'tivz) self-powered vehicles used to pull railroad cars
   *Example:* Steam-powered *locomotives* are now museum pieces.

**cylinder** (sil'ən dər) a solid shape having two equal-sized circles on each end and a smooth, curved surface between them
   *Example:* The cardboard tube inside a roll of paper towels is a *cylinder*.

**piston** (pis'tən) a disk or a cylinder that moves up and down inside a hollow cylinder
   *Example:* Steam pushed the *piston* up and down inside the steam engine.

**suction** (suk'shən) a force that sucks a substance (solid, liquid, or gas) into a space
   *Example:* The *suction* from the vacuum cleaner drew the dirt from the rug.

**engine** (en'jin) a machine that changes energy into mechanical work
   *Example:* A car's *engine* changes the energy that gasoline supplies into motion of the car.

### Academic English

**considerable** (kən sid'ər ə bəl) large in amount
   *Example:* The tornado caused *considerable* damage to the town.

**constructed** (kən strukt'əd) built
   *Example:* We *constructed* a new wooden fence to replace the battered one.

Answer the questions below. Circle the part of each question that is the answer. The first one has been done for you.

1. Does a *piston* stay in place or (move up and down)?
2. Would the force of *suction* push something away or draw it closer?
3. Does an *engine* change energy into mechanical work or into electrical wires?
4. Which is a *considerable* amount of money, ten dollars or ten thousand dollars?
5. Which is a *cylinder,* a pipe or a plate?
6. Which would a *locomotive* do, push a train car or be pushed by a train car?
7. If something were *constructed,* would it be torn down or built up?

**Dictionary** Now skim the article and look for other words that are new to you. Write each new word and its definition in the Personal Dictionary.

# While You Read

**Tip!** **Think about why you read.** Steam power made travel much easier and faster than it had been before. What is the fastest way that you have traveled? As you read, think about why people long ago might have wished to take faster trips.

CROSSING THE LAND WITH

# Steam Power

1    At the end of the eighteenth century, land travel was slow and difficult. Most people did not travel far or often. People walked, rode a horse, or took a horse-drawn carriage. Farmers could not send their crops very far to be sold at a market. Mail and supplies took a **considerable** amount of time to get from one
5 place to another. Then people began to build railroads and trains powered by steam **locomotives.** Steam power helped people and goods get moving.

   A steam engine changes steam energy to mechanical energy. Mechanical energy can be used to run many types of machines. The first steam engine was very simple. Water in a **cylinder** was heated until it boiled. Boiling water changes
10 to steam. Steam expands. The steam pushed up a machine part called a **piston.** As the cylinder quickly cooled, it created **suction** that pulled the piston back down.

   In 1698 a steam **engine** was made to run a pump in England. The pump drew water out of flooded mines. Then, in 1769, James Watt **constructed** a better steam engine. He developed it into one that used pistons to turn a wheel. It could power
15 many types of machines that used circular motion.

   Other English inventors made steam engines that could power vehicles. Richard Trevithick used a high-pressure steam engine to make the first steam locomotive. It pulled ten tons of iron and seventy men on nine miles of track. In just one trip, it proved that steam power could pull railroad cars. Later, in 1825, the first true
20 railroad came into use in England. It carried people and supplies on scheduled trips.

   The first railroad in the United States was the Baltimore and Ohio (B&O). Horses had been pulling cars on a set of tracks that had sharp curves. The B&O Railroad owners wanted to try steam power, but English trains were too big for the tracks. Peter Cooper built a smaller train called the *Tom Thumb.* In 1830 the
25 *Tom Thumb* made its first trip. Ten years later, there were more than two thousand miles of track in the United States.

   The railroads grew quickly. By 1869 they were running all the way from the East Coast to the West Coast. People, supplies, and mail moved quickly and safely. Steam power took trains over the rails across the land. Trips that had once
30 taken weeks now took just two or three days.

**LANGUAGE CONNECTION**

In the phrase "steam power," *power* is used as a noun. In the phrase "trains powered by steam locomotives," *powered* is used as a verb. What is a car engine powered by?

**CONTENT CONNECTION**

Diesel-electric locomotives came to North America in the 1920s, but not until the late 1950s did the diesel largely replace the steam engine. Guess which American railroad produced the first streamlined diesel locomotive.

# After You Read

## A. Organizing Ideas

**What were the effects of the invention of the steam engine?** Complete the chart below. In the left column, write down events related to the steam engine. In the second column, write down two effects of each event. Refer to the article for help. The first one has been done for you.

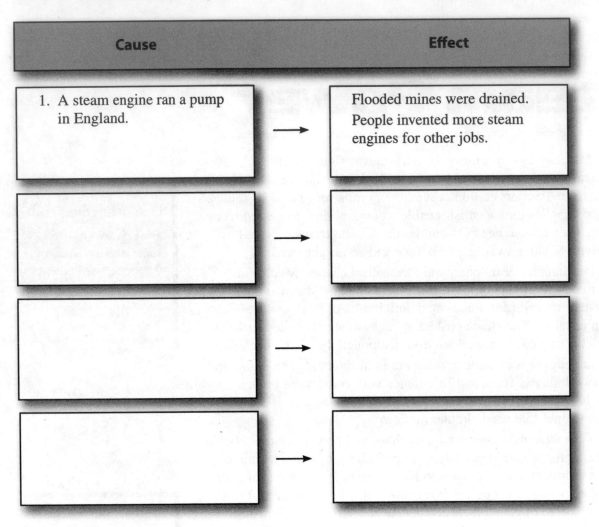

| Cause | Effect |
|---|---|
| 1. A steam engine ran a pump in England. | Flooded mines were drained. People invented more steam engines for other jobs. |
| | |
| | |
| | |

How does this chart show you the ways the steam engine affected England and the United States? Which effect do you think was most important? Write two or more sentences about it. How did this chart help you organize cause-and-effect relationships?

_____

_____

_____

_____

_____

## B. Comprehension Skills

**Tip!** **Think about how to find answers.** Look back at what you read. The words in an answer are usually contained in a single sentence.

Mark box **a, b,** or **c** with an **X** before the choice that best completes each sentence.

### Recalling Facts

1. At the end of the eighteenth century, land travel was
   - ☐ **a.** slow but easy.
   - ☐ **b.** slow and difficult.
   - ☐ **c.** fast and easy.

2. Steam engines change steam energy into
   - ☐ **a.** locomotives.
   - ☐ **b.** mechanical energy.
   - ☐ **c.** boiling water.

3. James Watt built an engine that could
   - ☐ **a.** turn a wheel.
   - ☐ **b.** change suction into steam energy.
   - ☐ **c.** power a car.

4. Richard Trevithick built the
   - ☐ **a.** B&O Railroad.
   - ☐ **b.** *Tom Thumb* train.
   - ☐ **c.** first steam locomotive.

5. Railroads replaced traditional means of travel such as
   - ☐ **a.** walking.
   - ☐ **b.** the bicycle.
   - ☐ **c.** the horse-drawn wagon or carriage.

### Understanding Ideas

1. From the article, you can conclude that English inventors
   - ☐ **a.** were smarter than other inventors.
   - ☐ **b.** developed the steam engine.
   - ☐ **c.** discovered steam.

2. You can also conclude that steam locomotives
   - ☐ **a.** were slow.
   - ☐ **b.** could pull heavy loads.
   - ☐ **c.** could do more work than fifty horses.

3. The B&O Railroad needed a smaller locomotive because
   - ☐ **a.** a smaller train could go all the way from coast to coast.
   - ☐ **b.** the curves in the B&O's track were too sharp for the big English locomotives.
   - ☐ **c.** horses could pull a smaller train more easily than a large one.

4. Factories produced more goods after the steam engine was invented because
   - ☐ **a.** coal mines could produce more coal.
   - ☐ **b.** factory workers could ride trains to their jobs.
   - ☐ **c.** factories began using machines powered by steam engines.

5. From the article, you can conclude that railroads grew quickly in the United States because they
   - ☐ **a.** were needed to move people and supplies long distances.
   - ☐ **b.** cost less to ride than horse-drawn carriages.
   - ☐ **c.** ran on tracks.

## C. Reading Strategies

### 1. Recognizing Words in Context

Find the word *expands* in the article. One definition below is closest to the meaning of that word. One definition has the opposite or nearly the opposite meaning. The remaining definition has a meaning that has nothing to do with the other two words. Label the definitions **C** for *closest*, **O** for *opposite* or *nearly opposite*, and **U** for *unrelated*.

_____ **a.** gets smaller

_____ **b.** gets bigger

_____ **c.** turns wheels

### 2. Distinguishing Fact from Opinion

Two of the statements below present *facts,* which can be proved. The other statement is an *opinion,* which expresses someone's thoughts or beliefs. Label the statements **F** for *fact* and **O** for *opinion*.

_____ **a.** Railroads were used in England before they were used elsewhere.

_____ **b.** English locomotives were more beautiful than American ones.

_____ **c.** Before steam power ran machines, people and supplies traveled slowly.

### 3. Making Correct Inferences

Two of the statements below are correct inferences, or reasonable guesses, that are based on information in the article. The other statement is an incorrect inference. Label the statements **C** for *correct* inference and **I** for *incorrect* inference.

_____ **a.** Inventors realized that steam engines were useful.

_____ **b.** Many people were injured by steam engines.

_____ **c.** The *Tom Thumb* pulled railroad cars more easily and safely than horses did.

### 4. Understanding Main Ideas

One of the statements below expresses the main idea of the article. Another statement is too general, or too broad. The other explains only part of the article; it is too narrow. Label the statements **M** for *main idea*, **B** for *too broad*, and **N** for *too narrow*.

_____ **a.** In 1769 James Watt improved the steam engine.

_____ **b.** Steam power made it possible to do many things.

_____ **c.** Steam-powered engines allowed people and supplies to move more quickly in the early 1800s.

### 5. Responding to the Article

Complete the following sentence in your own words:

Reading "Crossing the Land with Steam Power" made me want to learn more about

_____

because _____

## D. Expanding Vocabulary

### Content-Area Words

Complete each analogy with a word from the box. Write in the missing word.

| locomotive | engine | piston | cylinder | suction |

**1.** horse : wagon :: _____ : railroad cars

**2.** pot : soup :: _____ : water

**3.** steam : piston up :: _____ : piston down

**4.** wind : windmills :: _____ : vehicles

**5.** lightbulb : lamp :: _____ : cylinder

### Academic English

In the article "Crossing the Land with Steam Power," you learned that *considerable* means "large in amount." *Considerable* can also mean "important," as in the following sentence.

*His degree offered him considerable prestige in his neighborhood.*

Complete the sentence below.

**1.** People have created inventions of *considerable* value over time, such as _____

Now use the word *considerable* in a sentence of your own.

**2.** _____

_____

You also learned that *constructed* means "built." *Constructed* can also mean "drew (a geometric figure)," as in the following sentence.

*We constructed two triangles to compare in math class.*

Complete the sentence below.

**3.** When he *constructed* the blueprints, the design _____

Now use the word *constructed* in two sentences of your own.

**4.** _____

**5.** _____

Share your new sentences with a partner.

## Before You Read

**Tip!** **Think about what you know.** Read the first paragraph of the article on the opposite page. What is your favorite season? Read the article to learn more about the seasons.

## Vocabulary

The content-area and academic English words below appear in "Seasons Around the World." Read the definitions and the example sentences.

**Content-Area Words**

**seasons** (sē′zənz) times of the year related to a particular kind of weather
   *Example:* In some places the weather changes in each of four *seasons*.

**axis** (ak′sis) an imaginary line passing through Earth, around which Earth rotates, or turns
   *Example:* A globe turns around a pole that passes through its center, just as Earth rotates on its *axis*.

**tilted** (til′təd) leaning at an angle
   *Example:* After the car hit it, the stop sign became *tilted* but did not fall.

**hemisphere** (hem′is fēr) one-half of Earth, as divided by the equator
   *Example:* North America is in the Northern *Hemisphere* of Earth.

**solstice** (sol′stis) one of two times each year that the sun is farthest north or south of the equator
   *Example:* In the Northern Hemisphere, the summer *solstice* occurs in June, when the sun is tilted toward that half of Earth.

**Academic English**

**consequently** (kon′sə kwent′ lē) as a result
   *Example:* I saved my money; *consequently*, I was able to buy a new bicycle.

**areas** (ār′ē əz) regions
   *Example:* In some *areas* of the world, rain does not fall very often.

Rate each vocabulary word according to the following scale. Write a number next to each content-area and academic English word.

<u>4</u>   I have never seen the word before.

<u>3</u>   I have seen the word but do not know what it means.

<u>2</u>   I know what the word means when I read it.

<u>1</u>   I use the word myself in speaking and writing.

 Now skim the article and look for other words that are new to you. Write each new word and its definition in the Personal Dictionary.

# While You Read

**Think about why you read.** How many seasons are there where you live? Some people may think that every place on Earth has four seasons. As you read, find out if this is true.

## Seasons
### Around the World

1   The **seasons** of the year are spring, summer, fall, and winter. They bring changes in temperature and weather. They also bring changes in the length of days. On summer days, there are more hours of daylight than on winter days.

There are two reasons that the seasons and the hours of daylight change. The
5   first is that Earth moves around the Sun. The second is that the **axis** of Earth is **tilted.** Imagine Earth as a big ball with a line going through its middle. At the top of the line is the North Pole. At the bottom is the South Pole. The line is Earth's axis, on which it turns. Now imagine that the line is not straight up and down but tilted.

10  Picture the tilted ball of Earth as it moves around the Sun. Sometimes the top half, called the Northern **Hemisphere,** is tilted toward the Sun. At the same time, the bottom half, or Southern Hemisphere, is tilted away from the Sun. At other times, the Southern Hemisphere is tilted toward the Sun, and the Northern Hemisphere is tilted away from it.

15  The half of Earth that is tilted toward the Sun receives more of the Sun's light and heat. In this part of the world, it is summer. The half that is tilted away from the Sun gets less sunlight and heat. In this part of the world, it is winter. When it is summer in the United States, it is winter in Australia. The United States is in the Northern Hemisphere, and Australia is in the Southern Hemisphere.

20  The equator, or middle region, stays the same distance from the Sun all the time. There the temperature stays the same, and the hours of daylight do not change. **Consequently,** there are no spring, summer, fall, and winter seasons at the equator. However, the amount of rain does change. **Areas** near the equator have a wet season and a dry season.

25  What happens at the North and South Poles? The Sun shines all day at the start of summer. It is dark all day at the start of winter.

Once a year, in June, the Sun reaches its most northern point in the sky. In the Northern Hemisphere, this time is called the summer **solstice.** This day has the most hours of daylight. In December the Sun reaches its most southern point. This
30  is the winter solstice in the Northern Hemisphere, the day with the fewest hours of daylight.

**CONTENT CONNECTION**

The world can also be divided in half into the Eastern Hemisphere and the Western Hemisphere. North, Central, and South America are found in the Western Hemisphere. Can you name some places that are found in the Eastern Hemisphere?

**LANGUAGE CONNECTION**

Have you heard the words *solstice* and *solar* before? Both words are based on the Latin root *sol,* which means "sun." The Spanish word for *sun* is also *sol.*

# After You Read

## A. Organizing Ideas

**What do you know or want to know about the seasons?** Complete the chart. Write four facts you know, four facts you want to know, and four facts you have learned from the article about seasons. The first row has been done for you.

| What I Know | What I Want to Learn | What I Have Learned |
|---|---|---|
| I live in the Northern Hemisphere. | What does *hemisphere* mean? | A hemisphere is half of Earth. The Northern Hemisphere is the top half of a globe or map. |
| | | |
| | | |
| | | |

Did this chart help you learn more about a fact or facts that you already knew? Write two or more sentences about something new that you have learned. How would you be able to use this type of chart again when you read something else?

_____

_____

_____

_____

_____

_____

_____

## B. Comprehension Skills

**Tip!** **Think about how to find answers.** Read each item carefully. Underline the words that will help you figure out how to complete each item.

Mark box **a, b,** or **c** with an **X** before the choice that best completes each sentence.

### Recalling Facts

1. The reasons the seasons change are that
   - ☐ **a.** the North Pole is in the Northern Hemisphere, and the South Pole is in the Southern Hemisphere.
   - ☐ **b.** Earth moves around the Sun, and Earth's axis is tilted.
   - ☐ **c.** the Northern Hemisphere is tilted toward the Sun, and the Sun gives off energy.

2. Places near the equator have
   - ☐ **a.** four seasons.
   - ☐ **b.** a wet season and a dry season.
   - ☐ **c.** a light season and a dark season.

3. The Northern Hemisphere is tilted toward the Sun in
   - ☐ **a.** September.
   - ☐ **b.** December.
   - ☐ **c.** June.

4. In the Southern Hemisphere, it is winter in
   - ☐ **a.** June.
   - ☐ **b.** September.
   - ☐ **c.** January.

5. Australia is located
   - ☐ **a.** in the Northern Hemisphere.
   - ☐ **b.** in the Southern Hemisphere.
   - ☐ **c.** near the equator.

### Understanding Ideas

1. When the Northern Hemisphere is tilted toward the Sun, the Southern Hemisphere is tilted away from the Sun because
   - ☐ **a.** Earth rotates on its axis.
   - ☐ **b.** Earth's axis is tilted.
   - ☐ **c.** winter is colder than summer.

2. When the Northern Hemisphere is most tilted toward the Sun, it is
   - ☐ **a.** summer in New Jersey.
   - ☐ **b.** winter in New Jersey.
   - ☐ **c.** summer in Australia.

3. When the North Pole has winter, the South Pole has
   - ☐ **a.** summer.
   - ☐ **b.** winter.
   - ☐ **c.** spring.

4. In the Southern Hemisphere, the summer solstice takes place about
   - ☐ **a.** June 20 or 21.
   - ☐ **b.** September 20 or 21.
   - ☐ **c.** December 20 or 21.

5. In the Northern Hemisphere, it is light outside longest on the
   - ☐ **a.** winter solstice.
   - ☐ **b.** vernal equinox.
   - ☐ **c.** summer solstice.

## C. Reading Strategies

### 1. Recognizing Words in Context

Find the word *tilted* in the article. One definition below is closest to the meaning of that word. One definition has the opposite or nearly the opposite meaning. The remaining definition has a meaning that has nothing to do with the other two words. Label the definitions **C** for *closest*, **O** for *opposite* or *nearly opposite*, and **U** for *unrelated*.

_____ **a.** at an angle

_____ **b.** talented

_____ **c.** straight up and down

### 2. Distinguishing Fact from Opinion

Two of the statements below present *facts,* which can be proved. The other statement is an *opinion,* which expresses someone's thoughts or beliefs. Label the statements **F** for *fact* and **O** for *opinion.*

_____ **a.** When it is summer in the United States, it is winter in Australia.

_____ **b.** Cities near the equator have the best beaches.

_____ **c.** The hemisphere that is tilted away from the Sun gets less sunlight and heat.

### 3. Making Correct Inferences

Two of the statements below are correct *inferences,* or reasonable guesses, that are based on information in the article. The other statement is an incorrect inference. Label the statements **C** for *correct* inference and **I** for *incorrect* inference.

_____ **a.** The temperature is fairly predictable along the equator.

_____ **b.** On the winter solstice in the Northern Hemisphere, darkness comes earlier than on any other day.

_____ **c.** The South Pole is colder than the North Pole.

### 4. Understanding Main Ideas

One of the statements below expresses the main idea of the article. Another statement is too general, or too broad. The other explains only part of the article; it is too narrow. Label the statements **M** for *main idea,* **B** for *too broad,* and **N** for *too narrow.*

_____ **a.** Earth's position and movement affect the weather and amount of daylight in the world.

_____ **b.** On summer days there are more hours of daylight.

_____ **c.** Seasons are different throughout the world.

### 5. Responding to the Article

Complete the following sentence in your own words:
Reading "Seasons Around the World" made me want to learn more about

_____

_____

## D. Expanding Vocabulary

### Content-Area Words

Complete each sentence with a word from the box. Write the missing word on the line.

| seasons | Hemisphere | tilted | axis | solstice |
|---|---|---|---|---|

1. Earth's _____ is an imaginary line around which Earth turns.

2. The United States is found in the Northern _____.

3. The North and South Poles are at opposite ends of a _____ line.

4. The longest day of the year is the summer _____.

5. Earth's rotation explains why some _____ have more hours of daylight than others.

### Academic English

In the article "Seasons Around the World," you learned that *consequently* means "as a result." *Consequently* can refer to natural results, such as weather at the equator. *Consequently* can also refer to other kinds of results, as in the following sentence.

*My racket is broken; consequently, I cannot play tennis.*

Complete the sentence below.

1. The blue team had better players than the red; *consequently*, the blue team _____

Now use the word *consequently* in a sentence of your own.

2. _____

You also learned that *areas* means "regions." *Areas* can also mean "field" or "subject," as in the following sentence.

*He preferred the subjects of math and science to other areas of study.*

Complete the sentence below.

3. The critics focused on the *areas* of _____

Now use the word *areas* in two sentences of your own.

4. _____

5. _____

**Talk it Over** Share your new sentences with a partner.

## Before You Read

**Tip!** **Think about what you know.** Read the title of the lesson. Do you know the answer to that question? Think about what you already know about mammals. Read the article to learn the answer.

### Vocabulary

The content-area and academic English words below appear in "What Is a Mammal?" Read the definitions and the example sentences.

---

**Content-Area Words**

**monotremes** (mon′ə trēmz) mammals that lay eggs but produce milk to feed their young
    *Example:* A platypus is a *monotreme* because it lays eggs and feeds its babies milk.

**marsupials** (mär soo′pē əlz) mammals whose females carry their young in a pouch after birth
    *Example:* Kangaroos are *marsupials* that carry their babies in pouches.

**aquatic** (ə kwot′ik) growing or living in or near water
    *Example:* Unlike land plants, *aquatic* plants live in water.

**species** (spē′shēz) a class of beings that are related because they have similar characteristics
    *Example:* Human beings are members of the *species* known as *Homo sapiens*.

**pollution** (pə loo′shen) the process of soiling what is pure in nature
    *Example:* Water *pollution* occurs when large ships leak oil and chemicals into oceans.

---

**Academic English**

**consist** (kən sist′) are composed or made up (of)
    *Example:* Their dinners *consist* of a salad, a main dish, and fruit.

**function** (fungk′shən) act or operate
    *Example:* Our organs *function* in different ways: the heart pumps blood; the skin protects the body; the lungs draw air in and out so that we can breathe.

---

Do any of the words above seem related? Sort the seven vocabulary words into three categories. Write the words down on note cards or in a chart. Words may fit into more than one group. You may wish to work with a partner for this activity. Label the categories *Types of Mammals, Threats to Animals,* and *Other.*

---

Now skim the article and look for other words that are new to you. Write each new word and its definition in the Personal Dictionary.

## While You Read

**Tip!** **Think about why you read.** Do you have a pet, or do you know someone who has one? Do you know whether this pet is a mammal? Write a question about mammals that you would like to know the answer to. As you read, you may find the answer.

What Is a Mammal?

1  Mammals are warm-blooded animals that produce milk to feed their young. All of the 4,600 or so types of living mammals have backbones and hair. The largest mammal is the blue whale. This creature can grow to more than 33 meters (100 feet) long. Shrews and mice are the smallest mammals. Some are
5  less than 5 centimeters (2 inches) long.

Mammals live almost everywhere on Earth. They live in deserts, in forests, on grasslands, on mountains, and in water. Human beings, rats, camels, skunks, lions, deer, and wolves are all mammals. You may have other mammals in your home. Dogs, cats, and hamsters are mammals.

10  Almost all mammals give birth to live young, but a few lay eggs. These mammals are called **monotremes.** Even though monotremes lay eggs, they still produce milk to feed their newly hatched young. Monotremes **consist** of only two classes of animals. They are the platypus and two kinds of spiny anteaters.

Most mammals give birth to young that can live outside the mother's body as
15  soon as they are born. A few mammals, called **marsupials,** are not ready to do that at birth. Most marsupials live the first stage of life after birth in a pouch on their mother's body. Two kinds of marsupials are kangaroos and opossums.

Some mammals live in the water. These are **aquatic** mammals, or sea mammals. Some people think that dolphins and whales are fish, but they are sea
20  mammals. Sea mammals have lungs for breathing. Whales can hold their breath for up to thirty minutes. Whales and dolphins breathe through a blowhole on top of their heads. Whales and dolphins may look as though they have no hair, but actually they do have a few hairs on their heads or faces.

There are also other kinds of sea mammals. One is the manatee, often called
25  the sea cow. Manatees breathe through noses called snouts that they lift above the surface of the water. Seals and walruses are also sea mammals. So are polar bears, although they also **function** on land. Polar bears spend a lot of time hunting in water for food such as seals and fish.

About one-fourth of mammal **species** are threatened, or in danger of not
30  surviving. So few of these animals are left that they may disappear forever. Some of these species' habitats have been taken over by people. Some species have been poisoned by air and water **pollution.** Many have been hunted for food or for their skins. Several groups of people are working to save these species.

**LANGUAGE CONNECTION**

In the phrase "to feed their young," *young* is used as a noun. "Young" means "not yet adult." How else could you say "to feed their young"?

**CONTENT CONNECTION**

Lines 10–17 compare and contrast two types of mammals: monotremes and marsupials. Can you find other animals that are compared and contrasted in the article?

# After You Read

## A. Organizing Ideas

**How are monotremes and marsupials different from most mammals?** Complete
the diagram below. On the left, list facts about monotremes. On the right, list facts
about marsupials. Where the two circles overlap, list characteristics that all mammals
share. Use the article to help you. One item has been done for you.

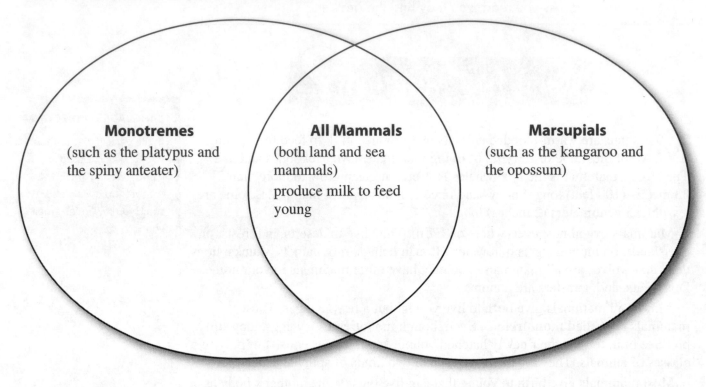

**Monotremes**
(such as the platypus and
the spiny anteater)

**All Mammals**
(both land and sea
mammals)
produce milk to feed
young

**Marsupials**
(such as the kangaroo and
the opossum)

How do monotremes and marsupials differ from other mammals? Write one or two
sentences about this difference. How will a diagram like the one above help you
remember what you have learned about mammals?

_____

_____

_____

_____

_____

_____

## B. Comprehension Skills

**Tip!** **Think about how to find answers.** Think about what each item means. Try to say it in your own words before you complete it.

Mark box **a, b,** or **c** with an **X** before the choice that best completes each sentence.

### Recalling Facts

1. Mammals
   - ☐ **a.** are warm blooded.
   - ☐ **b.** have no backbone.
   - ☐ **c.** are hairless.

2. Most mammals
   - ☐ **a.** lay eggs.
   - ☐ **b.** give birth to live young.
   - ☐ **c.** have pouches.

3. Mammals that lay eggs are called
   - ☐ **a.** monotremes.
   - ☐ **b.** marsupials.
   - ☐ **c.** shrews.

4. Whales and dolphins
   - ☐ **a.** lay eggs.
   - ☐ **b.** are fish.
   - ☐ **c.** breathe through a blowhole.

5. The largest mammal is the
   - ☐ **a.** kangaroo.
   - ☐ **b.** elephant.
   - ☐ **c.** blue whale.

### Understanding Ideas

1. From the article, you can conclude that mammals live
   - ☐ **a.** only on land.
   - ☐ **b.** only in water.
   - ☐ **c.** in most parts of the world.

2. From the article, you can conclude that you are a
   - ☐ **a.** marsupial.
   - ☐ **b.** mammal.
   - ☐ **c.** monotreme.

3. A newborn marsupial lives in its mother's pouch because it
   - ☐ **a.** is a member of a threatened species.
   - ☐ **b.** is not ready to live outside it mother's body.
   - ☐ **c.** would otherwise be eaten.

4. We know that opossums are marsupials because
   - ☐ **a.** they lay eggs.
   - ☐ **b.** they arc not fully developed at birth.
   - ☐ **c.** their young feed on milk.

5. From the article, you can conclude that polar bears
   - ☐ **a.** live only on land.
   - ☐ **b.** are a threatened type of mammal.
   - ☐ **c.** are aquatic mammals.

## C. Reading Strategies

### 1. Recognizing Words in Context

Find the word *produce* in the article. One definition below is closest to the meaning of that word. One definition has the opposite or nearly the opposite meaning. The remaining definition has a meaning that has nothing to do with the other two words. Label the definitions **C** for *closest,* **O** for *opposite* or *nearly opposite,* and **U** for *unrelated.*

_____ **a.** change

_____ **b.** destroy

_____ **c.** make

### 2. Distinguishing Fact from Opinion

Two of the statements below present *facts,* which can be proved. The other statement is an *opinion,* which expresses someone's thoughts or beliefs. Label the statements **F** for *fact* and **O** for *opinion.*

_____ **a.** All mammals have backbones and hair.

_____ **b.** A kangaroo is a marsupial.

_____ **c.** Manatees are the gentlest sea mammals.

### 3. Making Correct Inferences

Two of the statements below are correct *inferences,* or reasonable, that are based on information in the article. The other statement is an incorrect inference. Label the statements **C** for *correct* inference and **I** for *incorrect* inference.

_____ **a.** People often do things that threaten mammals' safety.

_____ **b.** A newborn kangaroo would probably die outside its mother's pouch.

_____ **c.** Mammals make the best pets.

### 4. Understanding Main Ideas

One of the statements below expresses the main idea of the article. Another statement is too general, or too broad. The other explains only part of the article; it is too narrow. Label the statements **M** for *main idea,* **B** for *too broad,* and **N** for *too narrow.*

_____ **a.** Sea mammals have lungs for breathing, so they must swim to the surface for air.

_____ **b.** Mammals may look different and live in many different places, but all have hair and backbones, and all produce milk to feed their young.

_____ **c.** Mammals live almost everywhere on Earth.

### 5. Responding to the Article

Complete the following sentence in your own words:

One thing in "What Is a Mammal?" that I cannot understand is

_____

_____

## D. Expanding Vocabulary

**Content-Area Words**

Cross out one word or phrase in each row that is not related to the word in dark type.

1. **mammals**      whale        skunk        iguana       lion
2. **monotremes**   eggs         platypus     anteater     shrew
3. **marsupials**   human beings kangaroos    pouches      opossums
4. **threatened**   endangered   increased    hunted       habitats
5. **pollution**    healthful    poison       water        air

**Academic English**

In the article "What Is a Mammal?" you learned that *consist* means "are composed or made up (of)." *Consist* can also mean "have a basis (in)," as in the following sentence.

*According to my father, a good life consists in staying healthy.*

Complete the sentence below.

1. Those artists' styles consist in the different ways they _____

Now use the word *consist* in a sentence of your own.

2. _____

_____

You also learned that *function* is a verb that means "act or operate." *Function* can also be a noun that means "use or purpose," as in the following sentence.

*The function of a piano is to make music.*

Complete the sentence below.

3. The *function* of a school bus is _____

Now use the word *function* in two sentences of your own.

4. _____

5. _____

**Talk It Over** Share your new sentences with a partner.

# Before You Read

 **Think about what you know.** Read the title of the article. Does your school have a science fair? Read the article to find out more about preparing a project for a science fair.

## Vocabulary

The content-area and academic English words below appear in "Organizing a Science Project." Read the definitions and the example sentences.

### Content-Area Words

**experiment** (iks per'ə mənt) an action or process designed to discover, test, or illustrate a hypothesis, or theory

 *Example:* Her *experiment* was meant to prove that beans grow faster than peas.

**accurately** (ak'yər it lē) done carefully with few or no errors

 *Example:* He scored high on the math test because he solved each problem *accurately*.

**hypothesis** (hī poth'ə sis) an idea based on facts that can be tested

 *Example:* The doctor formed the *hypothesis* that food caused the boy's sickness, but she called for tests to be sure.

**data** (dā'tə) information from which a conclusion can be drawn

 *Example:* The *data* for recent years proved that profits had steadily increased.

**conclusion** (kən kloo'zhən) a final decision, answer, or opinion

 *Example:* After driving for an hour, he came to the *conclusion* that he was lost.

### Academic English

**seek** (sēk) to search for (something)

 *Example:* In an emergency, you should *seek* help from someone nearby.

**affects** (ə fekts') makes (something) happen

 *Example:* The amount of rain *affects* how quickly plants grow.

Read again the example sentences that follow the content-area and academic English word definitions. With a partner, discuss the meanings of the words and sentences.

---

**Dictionary** Now skim the article and look for other words that are new to you. Write each new word and its definition in the Personal Dictionary.

# While You Read

**Tip!** **Think about why you read.** Have you ever been part of a science fair? As you read, think about how you would choose a topic for a science project.

## Organizing a Science Project

1 How can you create a great science fair project? You can start by asking yourself some questions.

1. *What is interesting to me?* You can connect almost any topic to science. Your topic could be plants, worms, dogs, the sky, or something else. If you cannot
5 think of a topic, search books or the Internet for ideas. **Seek** help from your teacher or a librarian. Your parents may have some good thoughts too.

2. *What question do I have about this topic?* A great science project always includes an **experiment.** Make sure that your question can be answered through an experiment. Here are some examples of questions: Does the
10 amount of light have an effect on how fast plants grow? How much salt is in different kinds of cookies sold at the store? Why does the sky change color at different times of the day?

3. *How much time do I have before the science fair?* A science fair to be held in two weeks will not give you time for some experiments, such as growing
15 plants. Carefully plan your project so that you allow enough time to perform your experiment **accurately.**

4. *What do I think is the answer to my question? Why do I think this?* The answer you choose is your **hypothesis,** or explanation. You will prove it right or wrong by performing an experiment. If you were to think about the sky
20 question, your hypothesis might be that the color of the sky is related to the position of the sun.

5. *How can I prove my hypothesis?* This is where the experiment comes in. You have to test your hypothesis. If you wanted to find out how light **affects** plant growth, you could plant seeds in a number of containers. Then you could
25 expose the plants to different amounts of light and compare the growth rates.

6. *How can I record my experiment?* If you were to do the plant experiment, you might measure each plant once a week and write the **data** on a chart. You could take photographs of the plants each week.

7. *How can I present my results?* You might display your question and
30 hypothesis on poster boards. You might then add pictures and graphs. A great science project also states a conclusion. A conclusion to the plant experiment might be *The plants that got the most light grew the fastest.*

When you have finished your project, you may have more questions. A great science project makes you want to learn even more.

**CONTENT CONNECTION**

Question 3 is about planning project time. People can plan for a party, a vacation, or a test. Why is it important to know how much time is available for an event?

**LANGUAGE CONNECTION**

The word *photograph* contains the /f/ sound as in *fish.* In what other word in this paragraph do the letters *ph* sound like *f* ?

# After You Read

## A. Organizing Ideas

**What are the seven steps for organizing a great science fair project?** Think of a project that you would like to prepare. Complete the chart below by writing down what applies to your project. List in order the seven steps for organizing a science fair project. Refer to the article to help you.

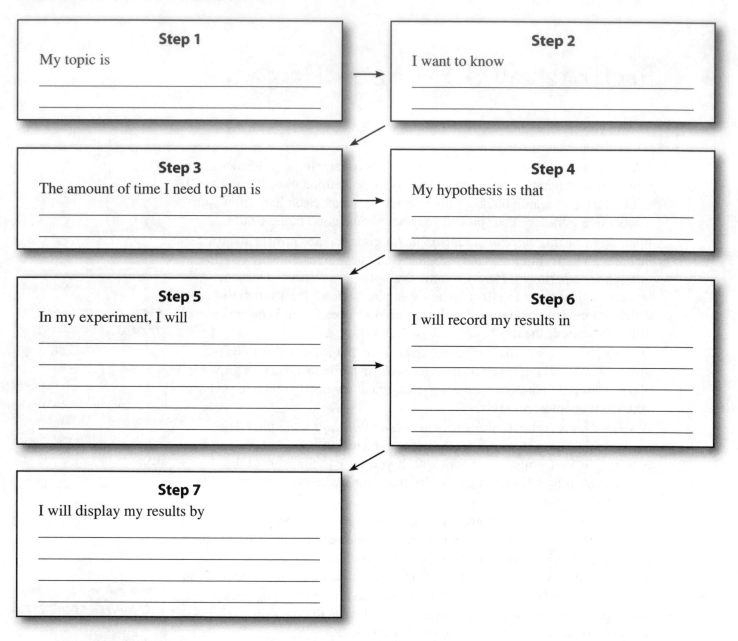

**Step 1**

My topic is

_____

_____

**Step 2**

I want to know

_____

_____

**Step 3**

The amount of time I need to plan is

_____

_____

**Step 4**

My hypothesis is that

_____

_____

**Step 5**

In my experiment, I will

_____

_____

_____

_____

**Step 6**

I will record my results in

_____

_____

_____

_____

**Step 7**

I will display my results by

_____

_____

_____

_____

Which step is the most difficult? Why? If you could not use this chart to help you prepare, in what other way could you organize this information?

_____

_____

## B. Comprehension Skills

**Tip!** **Think about how to find answers.** Look back at different parts of the text. What facts help you figure out how to complete the sentences?

Mark box **a, b,** or **c** with an **X** before the choice that best completes each sentence.

### Recalling Facts

**1.** One way to get an idea for a topic is to
- ☐ **a.** ask yourself what interests you.
- ☐ **b.** perform an experiment.
- ☐ **c.** make a display with poster boards.

**2.** A hypothesis is
- ☐ **a.** an experiment.
- ☐ **b.** a question.
- ☐ **c.** an explanation.

**3.** A great science project always includes
- ☐ **a.** an experiment.
- ☐ **b.** plants in pots.
- ☐ **c.** a number of results.

**4.** One way to test a theory is to
- ☐ **a.** draw a conclusion.
- ☐ **b.** make a hypothesis.
- ☐ **c.** do an experiment.

**5.** A great science project
- ☐ **a.** makes you want to learn even more.
- ☐ **b.** answers all of your science questions.
- ☐ **c.** raises many questions.

### Understanding Ideas

**1.** From the article, you can conclude that
- ☐ **a.** all science projects take about the same amount of time.
- ☐ **b.** some science projects take longer than others.
- ☐ **c.** science projects usually take about two weeks.

**2.** An experiment is an important part of a science project because
- ☐ **a.** it can be used to test your hypothesis.
- ☐ **b.** it can help you find a topic.
- ☐ **c.** it can help you think of a question.

**3.** To find out whether cold water freezes faster than hot water, you would first
- ☐ **a.** think of an experiment to give you the answer.
- ☐ **b.** state your conclusion.
- ☐ **c.** make a chart.

**4.** Performing experiments can help
- ☐ **a.** plants grow.
- ☐ **b.** you understand how things work.
- ☐ **c.** you form a hypothesis.

**5.** From the article, you can conclude that
- ☐ **a.** organizing a great science project involves several steps.
- ☐ **b.** all science projects should involve plants.
- ☐ **c.** a great science project starts with a conclusion.

## C. Reading Strategies

### 1. Recognizing Words in Context

Find the word *explanation* in the article. One definition below is closest to the meaning of that word. One definition has the opposite or nearly the opposite meaning. The remaining definition has a meaning that has nothing to do with the other two words. Label the definitions **C** for *closest*, **O** for *opposite* or *nearly opposite*, and **U** for *unrelated*.

_____ **a.** conversation

_____ **b.** answer

_____ **c.** question

### 2. Distinguishing Fact from Opinion

Two of the statements below present *facts*, which can be proved. The other statement is an opinion, which expresses someone's thoughts or beliefs. Label the statements **F** for *fact* and **O** for *opinion*.

_____ **a.** Experiments help test a hypothesis.

_____ **b.** Great science projects state a conclusion.

_____ **c.** Science fair projects about plants are the best ones.

### 3. Making Correct Inferences

Two of the statements below are correct *inferences,* or reasonable guesses, that are based on information in the article. The other statement is an incorrect inference. Label the statements **C** for *correct* inference and **I** for *incorrect* inference.

_____ **a.** Good science fair projects include experiments.

_____ **b.** Conclusions are based on the results of experiments.

_____ **c.** An experiment is used to test a conclusion.

### 4. Understanding Main Ideas

One of the statements below expresses the main idea of the article. Another statement is too general, or too broad. The other explains only part of the article; it is too narrow. Label the statements **M** for *main idea,* **B** for *too broad,* and **N** for *too narrow.*

_____ **a.** Organizing a science fair project involves following several steps carefully.

_____ **b.** Many hypotheses could be chosen for a great science fair project.

_____ **c.** The experiment itself is an important part of a great science fair project.

### 5. Responding to the Article

Complete the following sentence in your own words:

After reading "Organizing a Science Project," I want to write steps and plan for

_____

because _____

_____

## D. Expanding Vocabulary

**Content-Area Words**

Complete each sentence with a word from the box. Write the missing word on
the line.

| experiment    accurately    hypothesis    data    conclusion |

**1.** In my _____, I studied the effect of water on growing plants.

**2.** Then I recorded the information _____ on a chart.

**3.** I checked the results three times to make sure that my _____ was
correct.

**4.** This time my experiment proved that my _____ was wrong.

**5.** The science fair judge looked at my photographs, read my _____,
and praised my attention to detail.

## Academic English

In the article "Organizing a Science Project," you learned that *seek* means "to search
for (something)." *Seek* can also mean "to try to reach a goal," as in the following
sentence.

*People who seek high grades must study every day.*

Complete the sentence below.

**1.** Most athletes who go to the Olympic Games *seek* _____

Now use the word *seek* in a sentence of your own.

**2.** _____

You also learned that *affects* means "makes (something) happen." *Affects* can relate to
what happens in an experiment, as in the article. *Affects* can also relate to the result of
a cause, as in the following sentence.

*A hurricane affects people who live near the ocean.*

Complete the sentence below.

**3.** High heat *affects* water by making it _____

Now use the word *affects* in two sentences of your own.

**4.** _____

**5.** _____

**Talk It Over** Share your new sentences with a partner.

## Writing a Scientist's Travel Journal

Read the travel journal. Then complete the sentences. Use words from the Word Bank.

**Word Bank**

| | |
|---|---|
| areas | seek |
| marsupials | data |
| aquatic | |

**Friday, June 20**

**Dr. Yuk Ming Kwan**

Today I am traveling far into a place in Australia called the Outback. What a wild land! I have come here to _____ interesting and beautiful animals to study. Yesterday I saw kangaroos, the _____ that carry their babies in pouches on their bodies. I plan to visit lakes and rivers this week in order to study the _____ life there. I must be careful here, because many _____ in the Outback are dangerous. There are snakes, crocodiles, and other animals that bite! However, I must collect _____ so that I can learn more about this amazing place.

## Reading an Advertisement

Read the advertisement. Circle the word that completes each sentence.

# Take a Beautiful Train Ride up Snowy Top Mountain
## Enjoy Amazing Views!

- Take a ride to a height of more than 9,000 feet in one of our famous old (**conclusions, locomotives**). See the views from a comfortable seat with family and friends.

- Our powerful (**engines, monotremes**) will carry more than 100 people from the base of the mountain to our restaurant at the top of the mountain.

- Along the way, you will see beautiful forests full of rare plants and wildlife. Some trees on the mountain are (**accurately, threatened**) species. They may disappear from our world if they are not protected.

- Our trains are (**constructed, tilted**) so as to be completely safe. We have never had an accident in our 85-year history!

- The only (**alternative, hemisphere**) to taking our train is hiking up the mountain. (We think you will find the train more comfortable.)

**Buy your tickets now!**

 **Making Connections**

Work with a partner. Talk about what the words mean. How can you use the words when you talk about eating food? List your ideas in the plate and napkin shapes below.

| consume | fiber | disease | vitamins | nutrients |
| considerable | consist | consequently | function | affects |

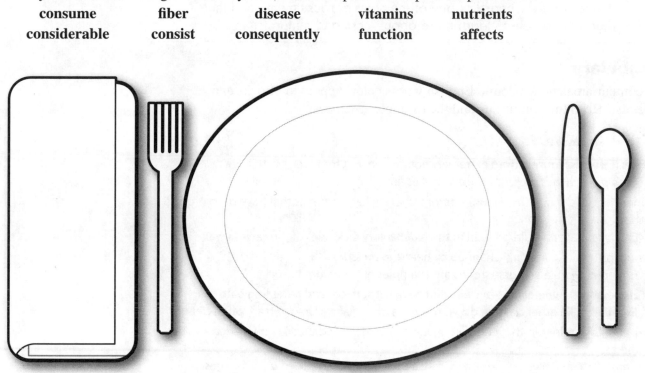

Use all of the words above in complete sentences of your own. Each sentence may include one or more of the words. To help you start writing, look at the ideas you wrote about. After you write your sentences, read them over. If you find a mistake, correct it.

_____

_____

_____

_____

_____

_____

_____

_____

_____

_____

# Before You Read

**Tip!** **Think about what you know.** Skim the article on the opposite page. Have you ever heard of any of the types of rocks mentioned there? Read the article to learn more about rocks and minerals.

## Vocabulary

The content-area and academic English words below appear in "Rocks and Minerals." Read the definitions and the example sentences.

### Content-Area Words

**igneous** (ig′nē əs) formed from extremely hot melted rock from deep within Earth
> *Example:* Igneous rock was once as hot as fire.

**sedimentary** (sed′ə men′tər ē) formed from layers of hard minerals that have been pressed together
> *Example:* Layers could be seen in the *sedimentary* rock sides of the canyon wall.

**metamorphic** (met′ə môr′fik) changed by heat and pressure
> *Example:* Marble and gemstones are examples of *metamorphic* rock.

**crystals** (krist′əlz) minerals, often clear, that have flat surfaces and repeating patterns
> *Example:* Like other *crystals,* diamonds have many flat surfaces and are often clear.

**metals** (met′əlz) minerals that conduct heat and electricity and that can be melted, molded, or shaped
> *Example:* Gold, silver, copper, and iron are *metals* that have been used for ages.

### Academic English

**definite** (def′ə nit) easy to see or identify
> *Example:* The object in the child's drawing had a *definite* roundness to its shape.

**significant** (sig nif′i kənt) having a strong effect
> *Example:* When the Sun came up, the change in the temperature was *significant.*

Answer the questions below. Circle the part of each question that is the answer. The first one has been done for you.

1. When an answer is *definite*, is it (clear) or unclear?
2. Is an *igneous* rock formed by heat or cold?
3. If a clue is *significant*, is it important or unimportant?
4. Which are found in *sedimentary* rock, layers or crystals?
5. Which is an example of *metamorphic* rock, rock that has changed or rock that has not changed?
6. Do *crystals* have smooth surfaces or rough surfaces?
7. Is it possible or impossible to change the shape of *metals?*

**Dictionary** Now skim the article and look for other words that are new to you. Write each new word and its definition in the Personal Dictionary.

# While You Read

**Tip!** **Think about why you read.** Do you like to put salt on your food? Salt is a mineral. As you read, think about other minerals you may have at home.

# Rocks and Minerals

1  When you hold a rock in your hands, you are holding a piece of our planet. Earth is made mostly of rock, which is just a collection of mineral pieces. All things in nature that are not animals or plants are minerals. Some minerals— such as salt, coal, and gold—are solid. This means that they have a **definite** shape.
5  Other minerals—such as water and natural gas—are not solid.

A geologist is a scientist who studies what Earth is made of and how it was formed. Geologists consider rocks in groups. The names of the groups tell how the rock is formed. **Igneous** rock is formed as hot magma cools. *Igneous* means "fire-formed." Magma is melted rock that comes from deep within Earth, where
10  the temperature is extremely high. Magma can harden and form rock if it moves higher up in the ground, where the temperature is cooler. Granite is formed this way. When magma rises to the surface in a volcano, it is called lava. Rocks formed from lava are called basalts. These are the most common kinds of igneous rocks.

15  **Sedimentary** rock forms when layers of hard minerals are stacked together. This can happen over time or from the force of water or wind. Two common kinds of sedimentary rocks are sandstone and limestone. If you look closely at these rocks, you can see the layers of minerals.

Sometimes **significant** heat and pressure are applied to igneous or sedimentary
20  rock. This may turn igneous or sedimentary rock into **metamorphic** rock. Metamorphic rock is rock that has changed its form. One example is marble. Like limestone, from which it is made, marble comes in many colors. Marble is much harder than limestone, however.

Geologists also separate rocks into groups according to how the rocks look.
25  They call some minerals **crystals.** Diamonds are crystals that are formed from a mineral called carbon. They are extremely hard. Graphite is another form of carbon, but it is soft. What we call lead in pencils is actually graphite. These minerals have different degrees of hardness. That is because of the amount of heat and pressure put on the carbon to make each one. Graphite is not the only soft
30  mineral. Another is talc, from which talcum powder is made.

Geologists refer to some minerals as **metals.** Iron is a metal. Most of the iron we use comes from the mineral hematite. Usually red, hematite may also be black with red streaks in it. The streaks are the iron. They are red because iron rusts when air and water come into contact with it.

**LANGUAGE CONNECTION**

Proper nouns start with capital letters. That's why "Earth" is capitalized. It's the name of one of the planets in our solar system. Can you name another proper noun?

**CONTENT CONNECTION**

Sandstone is a type of sedimentary rock. Why do you think it has this name? Sand is made up of tiny pieces of rock and hard minerals. As time passes, these pieces become pressed together in layers. The new stone is sandstone.

# After You Read

## A. Organizing Ideas

**What have you learned about three important types of rock?** Complete the chart below. In each column, write down two facts about the type of rock named in the heading. Refer to the article to help you. The first row has been done for you.

| Igneous Rocks | Sedimentary Rocks | Metamorphic Rocks |
| --- | --- | --- |
| These form when hot magma or lava (melted rock) cools. | These form when hard minerals are pressed together in layers. | These form when extreme heat and pressure are put on rock. |
| | | |
| | | |

What have you learned about the differences between these three types of rock? Write two or more sentences about these differences. How well did this chart help you organize facts about rocks?

_____

_____

_____

_____

_____

_____

_____

_____

_____

_____

## B. Comprehension Skills

**Tip!** **Think about how to find answers.** Look back at what you read. The information is in the text, but you may have to look in several sentences to find it.

Mark box **a, b,** or **c** with an **X** before the choice that best completes each sentence.

### Recalling Facts

1. The solid part of Earth is made mostly of
   - ☐ **a.** water.
   - ☐ **b.** rock.
   - ☐ **c.** sandstone.

2. Geologists group rocks according to
   - ☐ **a.** how the rocks are formed.
   - ☐ **b.** where the rocks are found.
   - ☐ **c.** the age of the rocks.

3. *Igneous* means
   - ☐ **a.** "layered."
   - ☐ **b.** "changed."
   - ☐ **c.** "fire-formed."

4. Sandstone is
   - ☐ **a.** igneous rock.
   - ☐ **b.** metamorphic rock.
   - ☐ **c.** sedimentary rock.

5. Diamonds are formed from
   - ☐ **a.** hematite.
   - ☐ **b.** carbon.
   - ☐ **c.** magma.

### Understanding Ideas

1. One example of a mineral is
   - ☐ **a.** a flea.
   - ☐ **b.** a fern.
   - ☐ **c.** salt.

2. A geologist would agree that all rocks are
   - ☐ **a.** formed in layers.
   - ☐ **b.** made of minerals.
   - ☐ **c.** formed by volcanoes.

3. From the article, you can conclude that
   - ☐ **a.** diamonds are harder than marble.
   - ☐ **b.** granite is harder than diamonds.
   - ☐ **c.** sandstone is harder than diamonds.

4. Under strong pressure, a layer of sedimentary rock can become
   - ☐ **a.** igneous rock.
   - ☐ **b.** iron.
   - ☐ **c.** metamorphic rock.

5. From the article, you can conclude that minerals are
   - ☐ **a.** always metals.
   - ☐ **b.** all around us.
   - ☐ **c.** found only in rocks.

## C. Reading Strategies

### 1. Recognizing Words in Context

Find the word *solid* in the article. One definition below is closest to the meaning of that word. One definition has the opposite or nearly the opposite meaning. The remaining definition has a meaning that has nothing to do with the other two words. Label the definitions **C** for *closest*, **O** for *opposite* or *nearly opposite,* and **U** for *unrelated.*

_____ **a.** floating

_____ **b.** liquid

_____ **c.** having a definite shape

### 2. Distinguishing Fact from Opinion

Two of the statements below present *facts*, which can be proved. The other statement is an *opinion,* which expresses someone's thoughts or beliefs. Label the statements **F** for *fact* and **O** for *opinion.*

_____ **a.** Metamorphic rock has been changed by heat and pressure.

_____ **b.** Basalts are rocks formed from lava.

_____ **c.** Igneous rock is more valuable than metamorphic rock.

### 3. Making Correct Inferences

Two of the statements below are correct *inferences,* or reasonable guesses, that are based on information in the article. The other statement is an incorrect inference. Label the statements **C** for *correct* inference and **I** for *incorrect* inference.

_____ **a.** Metals are more useful minerals than crystals.

_____ **b.** High heat and pressure turn a type of sedimentary rock into marble.

_____ **c.** Diamonds and graphite both are formed from the mineral carbon.

### 4. Understanding Main Ideas

One of the statements below expresses the main idea of the article. Another statement is too general, or too broad. The other explains only part of the article; it is too narrow. Label the statements **M** for *main idea,* **B** for *too broad,* and **N** for *too narrow.*

_____ **a.** Geologists study what Earth is made of.

_____ **b.** Most iron comes from a mineral called hematite.

_____ **c.** Earth is made up mostly of rocks that can be grouped according to how they are formed and how they look.

### 5. Responding to the Article

Complete the following sentence in your own words:

One thing in "Rocks and Minerals" that I did not understand is

_____

_____

## D. Expanding Vocabulary

**Content-Area Words**

Complete each analogy with a word from the box. Write the missing word on the line.

| metamorphic | igneous | crystals | metals | sedimentary |
|---|---|---|---|---|

**1.** ice : cold :: _____ : heat

**2.** minerals : salt :: _____ : diamond

**3.** metamorphic rocks : marble :: _____ : iron

**4.** igneous : granite :: _____ : sandstone

**5.** sedimentary : water or wind :: _____ : heat and pressure

**Academic English**

In the article "Rocks and Minerals," you learned that *definite* means "easy to see or identify." *Definite* can also mean "set" or "limited," as in the following sentence.

*Many people have a definite amount of time that they spend working each day.*

Complete the sentence below.

**1.** A square has a *definite* number of _____

Now use the word *definite* in a sentence of your own.

**2.** _____

_____

You also learned that *significant* means "having a strong effect." *Significant* can also mean "important" or "having great meaning," as in the following sentence.

*High school graduation is a significant day for students and their families.*

Complete the sentence below.

**3.** The most *significant* day of the year for me is _____

Now use the word *significant* in two sentences of your own.

**4.** _____

**5.** _____

**Talk It Over** Share your new sentences with a partner.

# Before You Read

**Tip!** **Think about what you know.** Read the lesson title above, and skim the article. Why do you think water is important?

## Vocabulary

The content-area and academic English words below appear in "Water Is Needed for Life." Read the definitions and the example sentences.

### Content-Area Words

**cells** (selz) tiny basic units of all living things
> *Example:* Every plant, person, and animal is made up of *cells.*

**urine** (yŏŏr′in) a clear yellow liquid waste released by the body
> *Example:* Our bodies release *urine* after we drink a lot of water.

**odor** (ō′dər) a smell or scent that may sometimes be unpleasant
> *Example:* Our noses told us that the *odor* in the area was from a skunk.

**pesticides** (pes′tə sīdz′) chemicals used to destroy harmful animals or plants
> *Example:* The farmer sprayed *pesticides* on his fields to kill the weeds.

**pollution** (pə lŏŏ′shən) items such as waste, garbage, or chemicals that make air, water, or soil dirty and can harm people, animals, or plants
> *Example:* The chemical factory caused *pollution* in the river that killed many fish.

### Academic English

**rely** (ri lī′) to depend (on) for help
> *Example:* The baby is helpless, and she must *rely* on her parents to care for her.

**obtain** (əb tān′) to get or gain possession of
> *Example:* At the store, we can *obtain* all of the food that we need for our trip.

Answer the questions below about the content-area and academic English words. Write your answers in the spaces provided. The first one has been done for you.

1. What word goes with *needing someone for help?* ___rely___
2. What word goes with *waste from the body?* _____
3. What word goes with *use your nose?* _____
4. What word goes with *millions in the body?* _____
5. What word goes with *kill insects that hurt plants?* _____
6. What word goes with *get what you need?* _____
7. What word goes with *dirty water?* _____

 Now skim the article and look for other words that are new to you. Write each new word and its definition in the Personal Dictionary.

# While You Read

**Tip!** **Think about why you read.** How do you use water every day? List the ways you use water. As you read, look for other ways people use water.

## Water Is Needed for Life

1   What would happen to a houseplant if nobody ever watered it? It would wilt and die. Animals and people need water too. In fact, all living things **rely** on water to survive.

    Why is water so important? It makes up most of the weight of living things.
5 An animal's blood and the liquid in plants are mostly water. Blood in animals and liquid in plants move food and get rid of waste. In the **cells** of plants and animals, important things take place. Cells cannot work properly without water—and if our cells do not work, we cannot survive.

    Our bodies lose water in many ways. We lose it through our skin when we
10 sweat. We lose tiny drops of it when we breathe out. We lose it in the form of **urine.** We lose between 2 and 3 liters (2.1 to 3.2 quarts) of water a day. In order to keep enough water in our bodies for our cells to work properly, we need to take in enough water to make up for what is lost. We **obtain** some water from food, but we get most of it by drinking. This is why people need to drink a glass of water
15 several times a day. On hot days, we sweat more, so we need to drink more. When the amount of water in the body falls below a certain level, we feel thirsty. Thirst is the body's way of making sure that we drink what we need.

    Think about the many other ways we use water each day. We use it to help us brush our teeth. We might use it to make soup for lunch. We add water to cake
20 mixes. We give water to pets. We water the grass and the flowers in the yard. When there is too little rain, farmers may need to water their crops. We take a bath or a shower to get clean. We wash our clothes and the dishes, clean the car, and mop the floor. We put out fires with water.

    Pure water has no taste or **odor.** However, chemicals, **pesticides,** and waste
25 from factories have polluted our water. Water **pollution** can cause health problems in people and can poison wildlife. The water that comes through faucets and water fountains is specially cleaned to make it safe to drink. Laws have been passed to prevent pollution. We need to do more to make sure that there will always be clean water for all of Earth's living things.

**LANGUAGE CONNECTION**

The words *liter* and *quart* apply to the measurement of liquids. We often abbreviate these words, or write them in a short form, as *l* and *qt.* What other abbreviations do you know?

**CONTENT CONNECTION**

Water is not the only thing that can become polluted. Can you think of other kinds of pollution that can damage our health or environment?

# After You Read

## A. Organizing Ideas

**How do we use water every day?** Complete the web below. In each circle, write down one way that people use water every day. Refer to the article to help you. The first circle has been done for you.

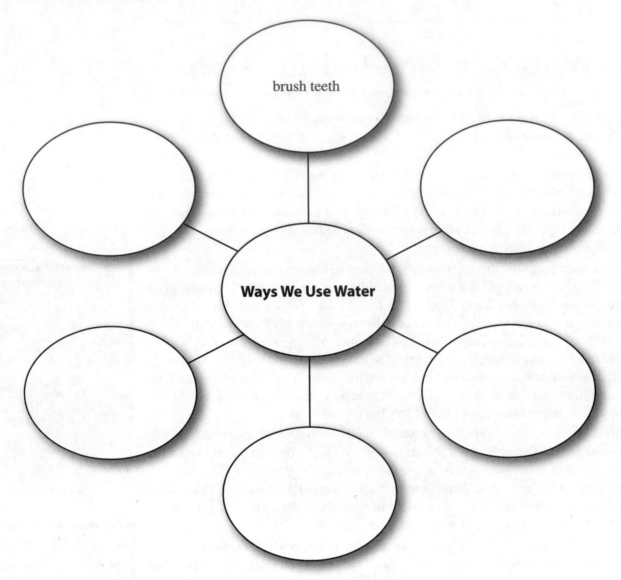

brush teeth

**Ways We Use Water**

Did completing this web remind you of our need for water? In what way? Write two or more sentences that describe the most important ways we use water. In what other way could you have organized the information that you wrote down on this web?

_____

_____

_____

_____

## B. Comprehension Skills

**Tip!** **Think about how to find answers.** Think about what each sentence means. Try to say it to yourself in your own words before you complete it.

Mark box **a, b,** or **c** with an **X** before the choice that best completes each sentence.

### Recalling Facts

1. Water makes up most of a living thing's
   - ☐ **a.** bones.
   - ☐ **b.** branches.
   - ☐ **c.** weight.

2. The amount of water we lose in a day is between
   - ☐ **a.** 2 and 3 pints.
   - ☐ **b.** 2 and 3 liters.
   - ☐ **c.** 2.1 and 3.2 liters.

3. When the amount of water in our bodies falls below a certain level, we
   - ☐ **a.** feel thirsty.
   - ☐ **b.** sweat more.
   - ☐ **c.** take a bath or a shower.

4. Blood and the liquid in plants
   - ☐ **a.** move food and help get rid of waste.
   - ☐ **b.** make up 90 percent of the weight of living things.
   - ☐ **c.** contain very little water.

5. Water pollution can be caused by
   - ☐ **a.** steam.
   - ☐ **b.** pesticides.
   - ☐ **c.** health problems.

### Understanding Ideas

1. Without water on Earth, there would be no
   - ☐ **a.** mice.
   - ☐ **b.** rocks.
   - ☐ **c.** deserts.

2. You would probably be thirstiest after
   - ☐ **a.** reading a book at the library.
   - ☐ **b.** watching television.
   - ☐ **c.** playing basketball on a hot day.

3. During dry weather, a farmer would consider it most important to
   - ☐ **a.** water vegetable crops.
   - ☐ **b.** wash the tractor.
   - ☐ **c.** use a hose to clean the sides of the barn.

4. You might think water were polluted if it
   - ☐ **a.** smelled bad.
   - ☐ **b.** had no odor.
   - ☐ **c.** had no taste.

5. Without water
   - ☐ **a.** some animals could survive.
   - ☐ **b.** most plants could survive.
   - ☐ **c.** no living thing could survive.

## C. Reading Strategies

### 1. Recognizing Words in Context

Find the word *survive* in the article. One definition below is closest to the meaning of that word. One definition has the opposite or nearly the opposite meaning. The remaining definition has a meaning that has nothing to do with the other two words. Label the definitions **C** for *closest*, **O** for *opposite* or *nearly opposite*, and **U** for *unrelated*.

_____ **a.** die

_____ **b.** live

_____ **c.** surf

### 2. Distinguishing Fact from Opinion

Two of the statements below present *facts*, which can be proved. The other statement is an *opinion*, which expresses someone's thoughts or beliefs. Label the statements **F** for *fact* and **O** for *opinion*.

_____ **a.** We lose between 2 and 3 liters of water each day.

_____ **b.** Animals like water less than people do.

_____ **c.** We get thirsty when our bodies need water.

### 3. Making Correct Inferences

Two of the statements below are correct *inferences*, or reasonable guesses, that are based on information in the article. The other statement is an incorrect inference. Label the statements **C** for *correct* inference and **I** for *incorrect* inference.

_____ **a.** We feel thirsty on hot days because our bodies lose water when we sweat.

_____ **b.** Without water, we could not prepare many common foods.

_____ **c.** The water we drink at home probably has pesticides in it.

### 4. Understanding Main Ideas

One of the statements below expresses the main idea of the article. Another statement is too general, or too broad. The other explains only part of the article; it is too narrow. Label the statements **M** for *main idea*, **B** for *too broad*, and **N** for *too narrow*.

_____ **a.** Our blood and the liquid in plants are made up mostly of water.

_____ **b.** All living things need water to survive.

_____ **c.** Clean water is necessary for life, and we use it in many ways every day.

### 5. Responding to the Article

Complete the following sentence in your own words:

Before reading "Water Is Needed for Life," I already knew

_____

_____

## D. Expanding Vocabulary

### Content-Area Words

Read each item carefully. Write on the line the word or phrase that best completes each sentence.

1. Without _____ the cells in our bodies cannot function.
   salt               water               blood               urine

2. We lose water through urine, the air we breathe, and _____.
   sweat              rain                thirst              fountains

3. We can _____ no odor in clean water.
   taste              see                 feel                smell

4. Our water can be polluted by the pesticides we use to kill harmful _____.
   pigs               diseases            insects             soil

5. The government has passed many _____ to protect our planet from water pollution.
   roads              laws                exams               constitutions


### Academic English

In the article "Water Is Needed for Life," you learned that *rely* means "to depend (on) for help." *Rely* can also mean "to have faith or confidence," as in the following sentence.

   *You can always rely on your mother to support you.*

Complete the sentence below.

1. I *rely* on my friends to be _____

Now use the word *rely* in a sentence of your own.

2. _____

You also learned that *obtain* means "to get or gain possession of." *Obtain* can be used when speaking of success in getting things. *Obtain* can also mean "to be accepted or customary," as in the following sentence.

   *Some customs, such as always wearing a hat in public, no longer obtain.*

Complete the sentence below.

3. The standards of polite _____ *obtain* at home or with friends.

Now use the word *obtain* in two sentences of your own.

4. _____

5. _____

**Talk It Over** Share your new sentences with a partner.

## Before You Read

**Tip!** **Think about what you know.** Read the lesson title above. Can you name a plant that has flowers? Can you name a plant that does not have flowers?

## Vocabulary

The content-area and academic English words below appear in "Flowering and Nonflowering Plants." Read the definitions and the example sentences.

**Content-Area Words**

**angiosperms** (an′jē ə spurmz′) flowering plants
  *Example:* The graceful shape of the tulip makes it one of my favorite *angiosperms*.

**pollination** (pol′ə nā′shən) moving pollen from the stamen of a flower to the carpels of the same or another flower
  *Example:* Sometimes bees help with plant *pollination* by carrying pollen from flower to flower while they gather nectar.

**gymnosperms** (jim′nə spurmz′) nonflowering plants whose seeds are found in cones
  *Example:* Pine trees are *gymnosperms* because pinecones hold their seeds.

**tracheophytes** (trā′kē ō fīts′) nonflowering plants that have spores instead of seeds
  *Example:* Ferns are *tracheophytes* because they have spores instead of seeds.

**bryophytes** (brī′ō fīts′) nonflowering plants that do not have roots, stems, or leaves
  *Example:* *Bryophytes,* such as mosses, are simple plants with very few parts.

**Academic English**

**process** (pros′es) several events or actions in a set order that lead to a result
  *Example:* Mother taught us her *process* for making shortbread.

**sufficient** (sə fish′ənt) enough to meet a need
  *Example:* We made sure that we had *sufficient* water for our hike through the desert.

Do any of the words above seem related? Sort the seven vocabulary words into three categories—Flowering Plants, Nonflowering Plants, and Other. Write the words down on note cards or in a chart. You may wish to work with a partner for this activity.

 Now skim the article and look for other words that are new to you. Write each new word and its definition in the Personal Dictionary.

# While You Read

**Tip!** **Think about why you read.** Have you ever seen or touched a pinecone? As you read the fourth paragraph, think about what gymnosperm seeds look or feel like in a pinecone.

# Flowering and Nonflowering Plants

1   People grow flowers to enjoy their beauty. We may enjoy just looking at flowers, but they are also useful. Flowers make seeds that can grow into new plants. Plants that have flowers are called **angiosperms.**

A flower has four parts that are arranged around its center. The outer part is a
5   circle made up of sepals, which are usually green and look like a ring of leaves below the petals of the flower. Sometimes the sepals are shaped like a cup. The part just above the sepals is a circle made of petals. Petals, which are larger than sepals, are the part of the flower you notice first. This is because they are usually either white or a bright color. Petals come in many shapes and sizes. Some petals
10  are separate, and others are connected to one another.

In the middle of the flower, just inside the petals, are the stamens. Stamens are thin strands that bend easily. They produce pollen. At the very center of the flower are the carpels, which make up the pistil. The seeds are produced in the carpels. For seeds to grow, pollen from the stamens must first enter the pistil. This **process**
15  is called **pollination.**

Some plants have no flowers but still produce seeds. They are called **gymnosperms,** which means "naked seeds." Their seeds do not grow in carpels. Instead, the seeds grow in cones, such as pinecones. Some gymnosperms are short plants; others are tall trees. Besides pine trees, the gymnosperms also include fir,
20  spruce, redwood, and cedar trees.

Another group of nonflowering plants, called **tracheophytes,** produces no seeds at all. Instead these plants produce tiny objects called spores. Ferns are tracheophytes. Ferns may seem to have long branches covered with short leaves. What look like branches are actually called fronds. On the back of a fern frond
25  are small brown bumps, called sori. Inside the sori, cells grow into spores inside enclosed cell cases. When it is warm, the cell cases dry out and break open. Carried away by the wind, a spore that lands where there is **sufficient** heat and moisture can grow into a fern.

**Bryophytes** make up another group of nonflowering plants. The best known
30  of these are mosses. These plants are unable to carry water and nutrients from one part to another. Each part must absorb its own water and nutrients. Most bryophytes live in wet, shady locations. Like ferns, mosses have spores rather than seeds.

**LANGUAGE CONNECTION**

When it is hard to understand what you are reading about, try to picture it in your mind. Picture the phrases *like a ring of leaves* and *shaped like a cup* to understand what sepals look like.

**CONTENT CONNECTION**

After reading the fifth paragraph, we can *infer,* or make a reasonable guess, that ferns grow in warm, rainy forests. Read the last paragraph. Where can you infer that bryophytes, such as mosses, grow?

# After You Read

## A. Organizing Ideas

**What have you learned about flowering and nonflowering plants?** Complete the chart below. In the boxes, list facts that you have learned about each type of plant. Refer to the article to help you. The first one has been done for you.

| Flowering and Nonflowering Plants | |
|---|---|
| **Angiosperms: flowering plants that produce seeds inside the carpels**<br><br>Pollination must occur for seeds to grow.<br><br>Tulips, violets, sunflowers, and irises are angiosperms. | **Gymnosperms: nonflowering plants that produce seeds in cones** |
| **Tracheophytes: nonflowering plants that produce tiny spores instead of seeds** | **Bryophytes: very simple nonflowering plants that have no roots, stems, or leaves** |

How did this chart help you learn about the ways different plants grow? Write two or more sentences about how nonflowering plants reproduce. In what other way might you have arranged this information?

_____

_____

_____

_____

## B. Comprehension Skills

**Tip!** **Think about how to find answers.** Look back at what you read. The words in an answer are usually contained in a single sentence.

Mark box **a, b,** or **c** with an **X** before the choice that best completes each sentence.

### Recalling Facts

1. The outer circle of a flower is made up of
   - ☐ **a.** petals.
   - ☐ **b.** sepals.
   - ☐ **c.** stamens.

2. Angiosperms
   - ☐ **a.** produce spores.
   - ☐ **b.** produce seeds but do not flower.
   - ☐ **c.** are plants that have flowers.

3. The seeds of gymnosperms
   - ☐ **a.** grow in carpels.
   - ☐ **b.** are spores.
   - ☐ **c.** grow in cones.

4. The word *gymnosperm* means
   - ☐ **a.** "naked seed."
   - ☐ **b.** "petals that are fused together."
   - ☐ **c.** "bright color."

5. Redwood trees are
   - ☐ **a.** gymnosperms.
   - ☐ **b.** angiosperms.
   - ☐ **c.** ferns.

### Understanding Ideas

1. From the article, you can conclude that
   - ☐ **a.** plants reproduce in different ways.
   - ☐ **b.** all plants grow from seeds.
   - ☐ **c.** all plants have flowers.

2. A tree with cones on it is sure to be
   - ☐ **a.** an angiosperm.
   - ☐ **b.** a gymnosperm.
   - ☐ **c.** a bryophyte.

3. The red part of a red rose consists of
   - ☐ **a.** sepals.
   - ☐ **b.** stamens.
   - ☐ **c.** petals.

4. Mosses grow best in rainy areas because
   - ☐ **a.** many ferns grow there.
   - ☐ **b.** they have no flowers.
   - ☐ **c.** they have no roots to take in water from the soil.

5. Brushing a finger across the stamens of a flower will probably
   - ☐ **a.** knock spores from the plant.
   - ☐ **b.** get pollen on the finger.
   - ☐ **c.** break open a cell case.

## C. Reading Strategies

### 1. Recognizing Words in Context

Find the word *notice* in the article. One definition below is closest to the meaning of that word. One definition has the opposite or nearly the opposite meaning. The remaining definition has a meaning that has nothing to do with the other two words. Label the definitions **C** for *closest*, **O** for *opposite* or *nearly opposite*, and **U** for *unrelated*.

_____ **a.** overlook

_____ **b.** destroy

_____ **c.** see

### 2. Distinguishing Fact from Opinion

Two of the statements below present *facts*, which can be proved. The other statement is an *opinion*, which expresses someone's thoughts or beliefs. Label the statements **F** for *fact* and **O** for *opinion*.

_____ **a.** The outer circle of a flower is made up of sepals.

_____ **b.** Pinecones should always be collected.

_____ **c.** Spores grow safely inside the sori.

### 3. Making Correct Inferences

Two of the statements below are correct *inferences*, or reasonable guesses, that are based on information in the article. The other statement is an incorrect inference. Label the statements **C** for *correct* inference and **I** for *incorrect* inference.

_____ **a.** There are more ferns than flowers growing on Earth.

_____ **b.** The petals of a flower are its most colorful part.

_____ **c.** Ferns and mosses do not need seeds in order to reproduce.

### 4. Understanding Main Ideas

One of the statements below expresses the main idea of the article. Another statement is too general, or too broad. The other explains only part of the article; it is too narrow. Label the statements **M** for *main idea*, **B** for *too broad*, and **N** for *too narrow*.

_____ **a.** Gymnosperms produce seeds in cones.

_____ **b.** Flowering and nonflowering plants reproduce in different ways.

_____ **c.** Living things must reproduce for their species to survive.

### 5. Responding to the Article

Complete the following sentence in your own words:

When I read "Flowering and Nonflowering Plants," I was reminded of

_____

because _____

_____

## D. Expanding Vocabulary
### Content-Area Words
Complete each sentence with a word from the box. Write the missing word on the line.

| pollination | angiosperms | bryophytes | gymnosperms | tracheophytes |

1. Among my favorite _____ is the pretty purple iris.

2. _____, such as ferns, grow well in rain forests.

3. Pine trees are _____ because their seeds grow in pinecones, not flowers.

4. During _____, pollen is transferred from the stamens to the carpels.

5. Each part of a _____ must absorb its own water.

### Academic English
In the article "Flowering and Nonflowering Plants," you learned that *process* is a noun that means "several events or actions in a set order that lead to a result." *Process* can also be a verb that means "to move forward slowly step by step," as in the following sentence.

*Will the graduates process, as a class, to music?*

Complete the sentence below.

1. The bride and her party will *process* _____

Now use the word *process* in a sentence of your own.

2. _____

_____

You also learned that *sufficient* means "enough to meet a need." *Sufficient* can refer to what a fern needs in order to grow. *Sufficient* can also be applied to other needs, as in the following sentence.

*Sufficient practice is necessary to become a good baseball player.*

Complete the sentence below.

3. A couple of blankets on the bed should be *sufficient* to keep you _____

Now use the word *sufficient* in two sentences of your own.

4. _____

5. _____

Share your new sentences with a partner.

# Before You Read

**Tip!** **Think about what you know.** Skim through the article. Do you think that recycling is an important thing to do?

## Vocabulary

The content-area and academic English words below appear in "Waste and Recycling." Read the definitions and the example sentences.

### Content-Area Words

**landfills** (land′fi_l_z) places where garbage is buried between layers of earth
   *Example:* The *landfill* area formed a huge hill.

**incinerators** (in sin′ə rā′torz) machines used for burning garbage or other waste
   *Example:* The *incinerators* for the cafeteria usually burned garbage after lunch.

**recycling** (rē sī′kling) preparing garbage to be used again
   *Example:* *Recycling* allows us to reuse old glass, cans, paper, and plastic.

**pulp** (pulp) a soft, wet mixture of paper and water
   *Example:* To recycle newspaper, hot water and paper are mixed together to form *pulp*.

**researchers** (rē′surch′ərs) people who study or investigate something, usually to learn new facts
   *Example:* The *researchers* are looking for new ways to recycle some kinds of plastic.

### Academic English

**items** (ī′təmz) objects or things
   *Example:* I found my hat, gloves, and scarf, and put these *items* into the closet.

**constantly** (kon′stənt lē) frequently; over and over again
   *Example:* The nurse was *constantly* at the patient's bedside, taking care of him.

Rate each vocabulary word according to the following scale. Write a number next to each content-area and academic English word.

4   I have never seen the word before.

3   I have seen the word but do not know what it means.

2   I know what the word means when I read it.

1   I use the word myself in speaking or writing.

 Now skim the article and look for other words that are new to you. Write each new word and its definition in the Personal Dictionary.

## While You Read

**Tip!** **Think about why you read.** Does your family recycle glass, paper, plastic, or cans? As you read, look for sentences that explain how these items are reused.

# Waste
### and Recycling

1  Each year people in the United States throw out more than 230 million tons of garbage. That is an average of about 2 kilograms (4.5 pounds) per person each day. Figuring out what to do with so much waste is a huge problem. Most of the waste is buried in **landfills.** Burying it gets rid of the trash but can create
5  other problems. Landfills can leak chemicals that pollute the land and water. Our landfills are filling up fast. In some parts of the country we are running out of places for new ones.

Not all of our waste goes into landfills. Some of it is burned in big furnaces called **incinerators.** The smoke from incinerators can pollute the air. The rest of
10 our waste is usually recycled. **Recycling** is making new things out of used things.

Paper is one of the easiest things to recycle. Some kinds of paper that are recycled are newspaper, cardboard, and paper that is used in offices. Newspaper that is recycled is mixed with hot water and turned into **pulp.** This pulp is mixed with a chemical that removes ink. The pulp is then made into new paper.

15 About two-thirds of the metal called steel can be recycled. Some scraps of steel are melted in furnaces and formed into sheets. The sheets can be used in making new cars, cans, and machines.

About two-thirds of aluminum drink cans are reused. The cans are crushed and then shredded and melted. They too can be made into large sheets from which
20 new cans can be shaped.

About one-third of all glass is recycled. Almost all of this comes from used glass containers such as jars and bottles. The glass is sorted by color into clear, brown, and green piles. Then it is melted and made into new glass **items.**

A small amount of plastic is reused. Plastic is harder to recycle than paper,
25 steel, or glass. Seven kinds of plastic are used to make household items, and each kind must be recycled separately. A number on the bottom of each plastic item tells what kind of plastic it is made of. Used plastic can be cleaned, shredded into flakes, and then melted and formed into small pieces. These pieces can be used to make new things.

30 Recycling is a good way to get rid of waste. **Researchers** are **constantly** looking for new, less expensive ways to recycle.

**LANGUAGE CONNECTION**

What does the idiom *running out of places* mean? It means "having very few places left." If you run out of something, you have none left. What do you think *running out of time* means?

**CONTENT CONNECTION**

Look on labels for the words *Printed on recycled paper* or *Made from recycled glass* (or *plastic*). Labels often include the words *Please recycle* to remind people not to throw items away. Why do you think that some people do not recycle?

# After You Read

## A. Organizing Ideas

**What happens to our waste?** Complete the chart below. List the benefits and problems connected with each way we get rid of waste. Refer to the article to help you. You may mention ideas of your own too. The first one has been done for you.

| Ways to Get Rid of Waste | Benefits | Problems |
|---|---|---|
| Landfills—places to bury trash | They help us get rid of a lot of trash. | They can leak chemicals that pollute land and water. |
| Incinerators—furnaces that burn trash | | |
| Recycling—reusing old things or making new things out of old ones | | |

What have you learned about the problems of getting rid of waste? Write two or more sentences about one of the waste problems. Did the chart help you organize facts in a way that made things clear to you?

_____

_____

_____

_____

## B. Comprehension Skills

**Tip!** **Think about how to find answers.** Read each sentence below. Underline the words that will help you figure out how to complete each item.

Mark box **a, b,** or **c** with an **X** before the choice that best completes each sentence.

### Recalling Facts

1. Each year the garbage produced in the United States comes to about
   - ☐ **a.** 30 million tons.
   - ☐ **b.** 230 million tons.
   - ☐ **c.** 550 million tons.

2. Landfills can pollute air, land, and water because they
   - ☐ **a.** are filling up fast.
   - ☐ **b.** can leak chemicals.
   - ☐ **c.** put smoke into the air.

3. Most used aluminum drink cans
   - ☐ **a.** are sorted by color.
   - ☐ **b.** cannot be recycled.
   - ☐ **c.** can be made into new cans.

4. The seven kinds of plastic used for household items
   - ☐ **a.** can often be mixed for recycling.
   - ☐ **b.** cannot be mixed for recycling.
   - ☐ **c.** must always mixed for recycling.

5. The amount of all glass that is recycled comes to about
   - ☐ **a.** one-third.
   - ☐ **b.** three-fourths.
   - ☐ **c.** one-eighth.

### Understanding Ideas

1. From the article, you can conclude that
   - ☐ **a.** every kind of thing can be recycled.
   - ☐ **b.** recycling cuts down on waste.
   - ☐ **c.** most things cannot be recycled.

2. One possible source of recycled steel might be
   - ☐ **a.** old cars.
   - ☐ **b.** dead trees.
   - ☐ **c.** brick houses.

3. One thing you might do to reduce waste is
   - ☐ **a.** throw away old newspapers.
   - ☐ **b.** use disposable plastic cups.
   - ☐ **c.** make a pencil holder out of a used jar.

4. The best way to deal with the problem of too much waste is to
   - ☐ **a.** build more incinerators.
   - ☐ **b.** recycle more used items.
   - ☐ **c.** open more landfills.

5. The item most likely to be recycled of these three is
   - ☐ **a.** a plastic ketchup bottle.
   - ☐ **b.** a glass pickle jar.
   - ☐ **c.** an aluminum drink can.

## C. Reading Strategies

### 1. Recognizing Words in Context

Find the word *expensive* in the article. One definition below is closest to the meaning of that word. One definition has the opposite or nearly the opposite meaning. The remaining definition has a meaning that has nothing to do with the other two words. Label the definitions **C** for *closest*, **O** for *opposite* or *nearly opposite*, and **U** for *unrelated*.

_____ **a.** costly

_____ **b.** exciting

_____ **c.** free

### 2. Distinguishing Fact from Opinion

Two of the statements below present *facts,* which can be proved. The other statement is an *opinion,* which expresses someone's thoughts or beliefs. Label the statements **F** for *fact* and **O** for *opinion.*

_____ **a.** Recycled paper is better than new paper.

_____ **b.** Recycling is the best way to get rid of trash.

_____ **c.** Recycled steel can be made into cars and machines.

### 3. Making Correct Inferences

Two of the statements below are correct *inferences,* or reasonable guesses, that are based on information in the article. The other statement is an incorrect inference. Label the statements **C** for *correct* inference and **I** for *incorrect* inference.

_____ **a.** Trash in landfills can make people sick.

_____ **b.** Plastic items are the least costly items to recycle.

_____ **c.** Incinerators can cause pollution.

### 4. Understanding Main Ideas

One of the statements below expresses the main idea of the article. Another statement is too general, or too broad. The other explains only part of the article; it is too narrow. Label the statements **M** for *main idea,* **B** for *too broad,* and **N** for *too narrow.*

_____ **a.** Newspaper is turned into pulp during the recycling process.

_____ **b.** Because it is good for our planet and helps reduce pollution, we ought to recycle as much of our garbage as possible.

_____ **c.** People create so much garbage every day that soon we will run out of places to put it.

### 5. Responding to the Article

Complete the following sentence in your own words:

What interested me most in "Waste and Recycling" was

_____

_____

## D. Expanding Vocabulary

### Content-Area Words

Cross out one word or phrase in each row that is not related to the word in dark type.

| | | | | |
|---|---|---|---|---|
| 1. **landfills** | bury | pollution | healthful | full |
| 2. **incinerators** | freeze | furnace | burn | air |
| 3. **recycling** | using again | glass | rock | steel |
| 4. **pulp** | newspaper | wet | ink | numbers |
| 5. **researchers** | study | learn | drive | scientists |

### Academic English

In the article "Waste and Recycling," you learned that *items* means "objects or things." *Items* can refer to things that are recycled. *Items* can also be used to refer to many other things, as in the following sentence.

　*A firefighter uses items such as a water hose and a ladder.*

Complete the sentence below.

**1.** *Items* on a pizza might include cheese, mushrooms, and _____

Now use the word *items* in a sentence of your own.

**2.** _____

_____

You also learned that *constantly* means "frequently" or "over and over again." *Constantly* can be used in a positive, or good, sense. *Constantly* can also be used in a negative, or bad, sense, as in the following sentence.

　*The neighbors constantly played loud music, disturbing us.*

Complete the sentence below.

**3.** Someone who *constantly* interrupts others _____

Now use the word *constantly* in two sentences of your own.

**4.** _____

**5.** _____

 Share your new sentences with a partner.

## Before You Read

 **Think about what you know.** Read the lesson title above. Do you know what an inventor is? Can you think of any famous inventors?

### Vocabulary

The content-area and academic English words below appear in "Elijah McCoy, Inventor." Read the definitions and the example sentences.

---

**Content-Area Words**

**inventors** (in ven′tərz) people who think of new things that make work or life easier, safer, or better
> *Example:* The *inventor* worked hard to build a safer kind of seat belt.

**engineer** (en′ji nēr′) a person who builds, repairs, or drives an engine
> *Example:* The *engineer* stopped the train so that he could work on the engine.

**device** (di vīs′) something created for a special purpose
> *Example:* We use that *device* to measure furniture.

**patent** (pat′ənt) a government document that prevents anyone but the inventor from making, selling, or using an invention for profit
> *Example:* He got a *patent* for his toaster invention so that no one could copy it.

**automatic** (ô′tə mat′ik) moving or working without outside help
> *Example:* An *automatic* door opens when you walk near it.

---

**Academic English**

**maintaining** (mān tān′ing) keeping (something) repaired and working well
> *Example:* He knew that by *maintaining* his car he would keep it in running order.

**acquired** (ə kwīrd′) got (something) through effort
> *Example:* She *acquired* many awards for the wonderful books she wrote.

---

Answer the questions below about the content-area and academic English words. Write your answers in the spaces provided. The first one has been done for you.

1. What word goes with *driving machines?* ___engineer___
2. What word goes with *working by itself?* _____
3. What word goes with *protects an inventor?* _____
4. What word goes with *toast bread in a toaster?* _____
5. What word goes with *thinking of new ideas?* _____
6. What word goes with *worked hard to earn something?* _____
7. What word goes with *keeping machines working well?* _____

---

**Dictionary** Now skim the article and look for other words that are new to you. Write each new word and its definition in the Personal Dictionary.

# While You Read

**Tip!** **Think about why you read.** What inventions do you use every day? Telephones, radios, and televisions were all invented by someone. As you read, think about your favorite inventions.

## Elijah McCoy | Inventor

1    Some people want to know how mechanical things work. They have creative minds and like to build new things. They might watch someone do a job and think of a way to make the job easier or safer. These people are known as **inventors.**

5    Elijah McCoy was an inventor. His parents had been enslaved in Kentucky. They ran away to Canada so that they could be free. McCoy was born in Ontario, Canada, in the early 1840s. He went to school there briefly until the family moved to Michigan. Soon he became interested in how machines work. His parents sent him to a school in Scotland when he was fifteen years old. There he studied to
10 become a mechanical **engineer.** Mechanical engineers design machines.

   While McCoy was in Scotland, the Civil War was being fought in the United States. After the war, McCoy went back to Michigan and got a job on a railroad. The managers of the railroad thought that an African American could not be a good engineer. McCoy accepted the less important job of **maintaining** trains.

15    McCoy kept the trains' steam engines working well. He oiled the moving parts of the train. It took a long time to oil a train. This job was dangerous because it had to be done while the train was standing still. When trains were stopped to be oiled, other trains sometimes crashed into them. McCoy invented a **device** that could oil a train while it was moving. In 1872 he applied for a **patent** from the
20 government to make and sell his **automatic** oiling cup. A patent is written proof that someone thought of a new idea or design.

   In less than ten years, the automatic oiling cup was being used in trains, ships, and many kinds of steam engines. McCoy moved to Detroit in 1882. There he thought up ways to make steam engines better. He also invented a folding ironing
25 board and an automatic lawn sprinkler. In 1920 he started his own business, inventing devices and selling them. He used the money he earned to improve his inventions. McCoy liked to show his work to children in his neighborhood. He urged them to go to school, and he hired young African American men to work for him.

30    McCoy kept on inventing things for the rest of his life. At the age of 80, he got a patent for a tire. In all, McCoy **acquired** 57 patents for his inventions.

**CONTENT CONNECTION**

Elijah McCoy's managers gave him a less important job than others because he was an African American. McCoy proved that race does not affect a person's ability to accomplish goals. What is one of your goals?

**LANGUAGE CONNECTION**

Inserting a prefix in front of a word creates a new word. The meaning of a prefix helps you understand the new word. The prefix *auto-* means "self." The word *automatic* describes something that works by itself. Can you think of another word with the prefix *auto-*?

# After You Read

## A. Organizing Ideas

**How would you describe Elijah McCoy's life?** Complete the chart below. In the boxes, write two or three facts about the early, middle, and late years of Elijah McCoy's life. Refer to the article to help you. The first box has been done for you.

---

**Early Years**

Elijah McCoy was born in Canada in the early 1840s.

He went to school in Scotland when he was 15.

He studied to be a mechanical engineer.

$\downarrow$

**Middle Years**

$\downarrow$

**Late Years**

---

What did this chart help you understand about Elijah McCoy's life? Write two or more sentences about what you have learned about Elijah McCoy. In what ways other than in the chart above could you record information about Elijah McCoy's life?

_____

_____

_____

_____

## B. Comprehension Skills

**Tip!** **Think about how to find answers.** Think about what each sentence means. Try to say it to yourself in your own words before you complete it.

Mark box **a, b,** or **c** with an **X** before the choice that best completes each sentence.

### Recalling Facts

1. People who have creative minds and build new things are called
   - ☐ **a.** Canadians.
   - ☐ **b.** railroad workers.
   - ☐ **c.** inventors.

2. McCoy applied for a patent for his oiling cup in
   - ☐ **a.** 1844.
   - ☐ **b.** 1872.
   - ☐ **c.** 1882.

3. When McCoy worked for the railroad, he
   - ☐ **a.** was an engineer.
   - ☐ **b.** took care of trains.
   - ☐ **c.** invented steam engines.

4. McCoy invented
   - ☐ **a.** the automatic oiling cup.
   - ☐ **b.** the steam engine.
   - ☐ **c.** patents.

5. McCoy started his own business to
   - ☐ **a.** make and sell his inventions.
   - ☐ **b.** repair steam engines.
   - ☐ **c.** build trains.

### Understanding Ideas

1. From the article, you can conclude that all inventors are
   - ☐ **a.** mechanical engineers.
   - ☐ **b.** educated in Scotland.
   - ☐ **c.** creative.

2. You can also conclude that McCoy
   - ☐ **a.** liked to do dangerous things.
   - ☐ **b.** liked to help other African Americans.
   - ☐ **c.** got rich through his inventions.

3. Of the following, the one that is not an invention is
   - ☐ **a.** plastic food wrap.
   - ☐ **b.** a can opener.
   - ☐ **c.** oil.

4. McCoy probably urged children to go to school so that they could
   - ☐ **a.** get better jobs when they grew up.
   - ☐ **b.** work for the railroad.
   - ☐ **c.** travel to Scotland.

5. An inventor walking a dog that kept getting tangled in its leash might
   - ☐ **a.** let the dog run free.
   - ☐ **b.** invent a new kind of dog leash.
   - ☐ **c.** scold the dog.

## C. Reading Strategies

### 1. Recognizing Words in Context

Find the word *creative* in the article. One definition below is closest to the meaning of that word. One definition has the opposite or nearly the opposite meaning. The remaining definition has a meaning that has nothing to do with the other two words. Label the definitions **C** for *closest*, **O** for *opposite* or *nearly opposite*, and **U** for *unrelated*.

_____ **a.** joyful

_____ **b.** full of imagination

_____ **c.** lacking in new ideas

### 2. Distinguishing Fact from Opinion

Two of the statements below present *facts*, which can be proved. The other statement is an *opinion*, which expresses someone's thoughts or beliefs. Label the statements **F** for *fact* and **O** for *opinion*.

_____ **a.** The airplane is the greatest machine that has ever been invented.

_____ **b.** Before the automatic oiling cup was invented, trains had to be stopped to be oiled.

_____ **c.** Elijah McCoy's first invention was an automatic oiling cup.

### 3. Making Correct Inferences

Two of the statements below are correct *inferences*, or reasonable guesses, that are based on information in the article. The other statement is an incorrect inference. Label the statements **C** for *correct* inference and **I** for *incorrect* inference.

_____ **a.** Inventors are curious and creative.

_____ **b.** Inventors are allowed only a certain number of patents.

_____ **c.** A mechanical engineer might work in a factory that builds new machines.

### 4. Understanding Main Ideas

One of the statements below expresses the main idea of the article. Another statement is too general, or too broad. The other explains only part of the article; it is too narrow. Label the statements **M** for *main idea*, **B** for *too broad*, and **N** for *too narrow*.

_____ **a.** Elijah McCoy was an African American inventor who created many important devices in his lifetime.

_____ **b.** Inventors such as Elijah McCoy are curious about how machines work and like to build new things.

_____ **c.** Elijah McCoy hired African American men to work for him.

### 5. Responding to the Article

Complete the following sentence in your own words:

Reading "Elijah McCoy, Inventor" made me want to learn more about

_____

because _____

## D. Expanding Vocabulary

### Content-Area Words

Read each item carefully. Write on the line the word or phrase that best completes each sentence.

1. Inventors enjoy thinking of new _____ to help people.
   recipes         devices        books        instruments

2. A mechanical engineer likes to _____ machines.
   repair         clean        destroy        design

3. A helpful device that makes cooking easier is a _____.
   microwave oven    toilet        camera        television set

4. An inventor who has a patent from the government is the only one allowed to _____ the invention.
   paint        bury        build        wear

5. An automatic dishwasher washes dishes _____.
   late        by itself        today        early

### Academic English

In the article "Elijah McCoy, Inventor," you learned that *maintaining* means "keeping (something) repaired and working well." *Maintaining* can also mean "continuing," as in the following sentence.

*Maintaining a safe speed when driving is important.*

Complete the sentence below.

1. *Maintaining* good study habits will help students earn _____

Now use the word *maintaining* in a sentence of your own.

2. _____

_____

You also learned that *acquired* means "got (something) through effort." *Acquired* can relate to how Elijah McCoy got his patents. *Acquired* can also mean "got through various means," as in the following sentence.

*He acquired the illness through contact with someone who had it.*

Complete the sentence below.

3. The young man *acquired* his house when the owner _____

Now use the word *acquired* in two sentences of your own.

4. _____

5. _____

Talk It Over  Share your new sentences with a partner.

## Writing a Journal Entry

Read the journal entry. Then complete the sentences. Use words from the Word Bank.

**Word Bank**
sedimentary    sufficient
crystals    rely    obtain

Tuesday, April 25

Omar Ali

Today was our school field trip to explore Cold Creek Cave. My science teacher wanted us to see some of the things we had studied in class. We had to _____ a note from our parents saying that we were allowed to go. I'm glad I did, because the cave was amazing! It had many kinds of rocks, including the layered _____ rock. I really liked the clear, shiny _____ we saw deep within the cave. Once we had traveled far into the cave, there was not _____ light to see. We had to _____ on flashlights to find our way. I enjoyed my trip to the cave.

## Reading an Interview

Read the interview. Circle the word that best completes each sentence.

# Daily News • Science

# An Interview with Our Student Scientist

### by Maya Chopra

I feel lucky to have had the chance to interview Joe Figueroa, a student here at our school. Joe has been studying the **(process, engineer)** of how bees help flowering plants bloom. Here is his interesting story.

*Maya:* Joe, tell me about what you have been studying.

*Joe:* I have been studying **(pollination, maintaining)**, how pollen gets from one flower to another. **(Pulp, Pesticides)** used to destroy insects create serious problems. The chemicals stop bees from carrying pollen to flowers.

*Maya:* What happens when bees do not move pollen?

*Joe:* Many **(acquired, angiosperms)**, or flowering plants, do not produce seeds.

*Maya:* What can you do with what you have learned?

*Joe:* I have passed on my information to **(researchers, patents)** at our state university. They will publish a paper that may help stop the use of harmful chemicals.

*Maya:* Congratulations, Joe! We're proud of you.

 **Making Connections**

Work with a partner. Talk about what the words mean. Write down words that fit in one of the columns in the chart below. Not all of the words will apply to one of the headings, but the same word may be placed in both columns. You may use the words alone or as part of a phrase or a sentence.

| definite | significant | odor | pollution | landfills |
| incinerators | recycling | items | inventors | device |

| Things That Are Good for Earth | Things That Are Bad for Earth |
| --- | --- |
|  |  |
|  |  |
|  |  |
|  |  |
|  |  |
|  |  |

Use all of the words above in complete sentences of your own. Explain why each word can be thought of as good or bad for Earth. To help you start writing, think about the groups of words you created. After you write your sentences, read them over. If you find a mistake, correct it.

_____

_____

_____

_____

_____

# Glossary

## A

**accurately** (ak′yər it lē) done carefully with few or no errors [15]

***acquired** (ə kwīrd′) got (something) through effort [20]

***affects** (ə fekts′) makes (something) happen [15]

***alternative** (ôl tur′nə tiv) a possible choice between items [11]

**altostratus** (al′tō strat′əs) describing a light gray layer of clouds found in the middle of the atmosphere [10]

***analyzed** (a′nə līzd′) studied (something) carefully to learn how it works [9]

**angiosperms** (an′jē ə spurmz′) flowering plants [18]

**aquatic** (ə kwot′ik) growing or living in or near water [14]

***areas** (ār′ē əz) regions [13]

**automatic** (ô′tə mat′ik) moving or working without outside help [20]

***available** (ə vā′lə bəl) possible to have or find [2]

**axis** (ak′sis) an imaginary line passing through Earth, around which Earth rotates, or turns [13]

## B

***benefits** (ben′ə fits) is helpful to [7]

**bryophytes** (brī′ō fīts′) plants that do not have roots, stems, or leaves [18]

## C

**cables** (kā′bəlz) strong, thick, heavy steel or fiber ropes [1]

**canopy** (kan′ə pē) overhead shelter or covering [2]

**cells** (selz) tiny basic units of all living things [17]

**cirrus** (sir′əs) describing thin white clouds made of ice crystals found high above Earth [10]

***complex** (kəm′pleks) having many related parts that work together [7]

**conclusion** (kən kloo′zhən) a final decision, answer, or opinion [15]

***consequently** (kon′sə kwent′lē) as a result [13]

***considerable** (kən sid′ər ə bəl) large in amount [12]

***consist** (kən sist′) are composed or made up (of) [14]

***constantly** (kon′stənt lē) frequently; over and over again [19]

**constellations** (kon′ste lā′shənz) groups of stars often named after characters or objects in myths [3]

***constructed** (kən strukt′əd) built [12]

***consume** (kən soom′) to eat [11]

**cotton** (kot′ən) fluffy fibers that grow in a fluffy mass in large seed pods on certain plants [4]

***create** (krē āt′) to cause to be [1]

**crystals** (krist′əlz) minerals, often clear, that have flat surfaces and repeating patterns [16]

**cumulonimbus** (kū′myə lō nim′bəs) describing cumulus clouds that rise upward like a tower and often bring thunderstorms [10]

**currents** (kur′ənts) streams of air, water, or electricity that flow in a certain direction [9]

**cylinder** (sil′ən dər) a solid shape having two equal-sized circles at the ends and a smooth, curved surface between them [12]

## D

**data** (dā′tə) information from which a conclusion can be drawn [15]

**deciduous** (di sij′oo əs) known for shedding its leaves every year [2]

***definite** (def′ə nit) easy to see or identify [16]

***derived** (də rīvd′) obtained or gotten (from something else) [4]

***design** (di zīn′) plan or make something for a purpose [8]

**device** (di vīs′) something created for a special purpose [20]

**dipper** (dip′ər) a long-handled cup or bowl used for scooping up liquids [3]

**direction** (di rek′shən) a line or path along which something moves, faces, or lies [3]

**disease** (di zēz′) an infection or illness caused by bacteria, viruses, or the body's failure to work properly [11]

## E

**electricity** (ə lek′tris′ə tē) energy that is capable of producing light, heat, and other effects [4]

**energy** (en′ər jē) power applied forcefully in order to do work [1]

**engine** (en′jin) a machine that changes energy into mechanical work [12]

**engineer** (en′ji nēr′) a person who builds, repairs, or drives an engine [20]

***environments** (en vī′rən mənts) the world around a plant or an animal that affects its life and growth [2]

---

\* Academic English word

Lesson numbers appear in brackets.

**equator** (i kwā′tər) an imaginary line circling Earth halfway between the North and South Poles [2]

**erosion** (i rō′zhən) the slow wearing or washing away, smoothing, and shaping of soil and rock [6]

**experiment** (iks per′ə mənt) an action designed to discover or inform about something or to test an idea [8, 15]

## F

**fiber** (fī′bər) plant material that cannot be digested by the body and so helps push waste from the body during digestion [11]

**fog** (fôg) small water droplets that hang in the air close to Earth's surface, making the air look smoky [10]

**forecasts** (fôr′kasts) guesses about something in the future, such as weather information [8]

**fuel** (fū′əl) material such as coal, wood, or oil that can be burned to produce power [1]

**fulcrum** (fool′krəm) a support, or point of support, on which a lever rests [7]

*__function__ (fungk′shən) act or operate [14]

## G

**grains** (grānz) edible seeds or seedlike fruits of plants such as rye, wheat, or corn [4]

**gravity** (grav′ə tē) the pull or force that Earth puts on things at or near its surface [1]

**gymnosperms** (jim′nə spurmz′) nonflowering plants whose seeds are found in cones [18]

## H

**hemisphere** (hem′is fēr) one-half of Earth, as divided by the equator [13]

**hypothesis** (hī poth′ə sis) an idea based on facts that can be tested [15]

## I

*__identify__ (ī den′tə fī) recognize or discover what something is [9]

**igneous** (ig′nē əs) formed from extremely hot melted rock from deep within Earth [16]

**incinerators** (in sin′ə rā′tərz) machines used for burning garbage or other waste [19]

**inclined plane** (in klīnd′ plān) any flat, sloped surface [7]

**injuries** (in′jər ēz) damage to the body of a person or an animal [5]

**intensify** (in ten′sə fī) make stronger [9]

**inventor** (in ven′tər) a person who creates new things to improve life, work, or safety [8, 20]

*__items__ (ī′temz) objects or things [19]

## L

**landfills** (land′filz) places where garbage is buried between layers of earth [19]

*__layer__ (lā′ər) one thickness laid over or under another [1]

**lever** (lēv′ər) a solid bar used to apply force at one end of something [7]

**lithosphere** (lith′ə sfēr′) the layer of rock on which all of Earth's land and oceans rest [6]

*__located__ (lō′kāt əd) settled in a certain place [10]

**locomotives** (lō′kə mō′tivz) self-powered vehicles used to pull railroad cars [12]

## M

**machine** (mə shēn′) a combination of parts that use forces, motion, and energy to do specialized work [7]

**magma** (mag′mə) melted rock beneath Earth's surface [6]

*__maintaining__ (mān tān′ing) keeping (something) repaired and working well [20]

*__major__ (mā′jər) great or large [3]

**mammals** (mam′əlz) warm-blooded animals that give birth to live young and produce milk [9]

**marsupials** (mär soo′pē əlz) mammals whose females carry their young in a pouch after birth [14]

**metals** (met′əlz) minerals that conduct heat and electricity and that can be melted, molded, or shaped [16]

**metamorphic** (met′ə môr′fik) changed by heat and pressure [16]

*__minor__ (mī′nər) small [3]

**monotremes** (mon′ə trēmz) mammals that lay eggs but produce milk to feed their young [14]

**myths** (miths) traditional stories about gods and heroes that express beliefs [3]

## N

**nutrients** (noo′trē ənts) nutritious substances, such as minerals and vitamins, that help the body function [11]

---

* Academic English word                Lesson numbers appear in brackets.

## O

**\*obtain** (əb tān′) to get or gain possession of [17]

**\*occurs** (ə kurz′) appears or happens [6]

**odor** (ō′dər) a smell or scent that may sometimes be unpleasant [17]

## P

**patent** (pat′ənt) a government document that prevents anyone but the inventor from making, selling, or using an invention for profit [20]

**patients** (pā′shənts) people or animals that are helped by a doctor or a veterinarian [5]

**pesticides** (pes′tə sīdz′) chemicals used to destroy harmful animals or plants [17]

**petroleum** (pə trō′lē əm) a flammable liquid made by nature deep beneath Earth's surface [4]

**phytochemicals** (fī′tō kem′i kəlz) substances found in plants that help the body stay healthy [11]

**piston** (pis′tən) a disk or a cylinder that moves up and down inside a hollow cylinder [12]

**plastic** (plas′tik) material, made from petroleum, that can be molded or shaped when soft [4]

**plates** (plāts) huge pieces of rock that make up the landmasses on Earth [6]

**pollination** (pol′ə nā′shən) moving pollen from the stamen of a flower to the carpels of the same or another flower [18]

**pollution** (pə lōō′shən) the process of soiling what is pure in nature [14]; items such as waste, garbage, or chemicals that make air, water, or soil dirty and can harm people, animals, or plants [17]

**primitive** (prim′ə tiv) crude or simple, not fancy [9]

**\*process** (pros′es) several events or actions in a set order that lead to a result [18]

**pulley** (pool′ē) a grooved wheel along which a rope or chain is pulled, often to move heavy loads [7]

**pulp** (pulp) a soft, wet mixture of paper and water [19]

## R

**recycling** (rē sī′kling) preparing garbage to be used again [19]

**\*rely** (ri lī′) to depend (on) for help [17]

**\*remove** (ri mōōv′) to take away [5]

**\*requires** (ri kwīrz′) makes necessary [5]

**researchers** (rē′surch′ərz) people who study or investigate something, usually to learn new facts [19]

## S

**scavengers** (skav′in jərz) animals that feed on dead or decaying plants or animals [9]

**scientists** (sī′ən tists) experts in one of the sciences [8]

**seasons** (sē′zənz) times of the year related to a particular kind of weather [13]

**\*sections** (sek′shənz) parts that are cut off or separated from other parts [6]

**sedimentary** (sed′ə men′tər ē) formed from layers of hard minerals that have been pressed together [16]

**\*seek** (sēk) to search for (something) [15]

**\*significant** (sig nif′i kənt) having a strong effect [16]

**\*similar** (sim′ə lər) like something else [8]

**solstice** (sol′stis) one of two times each year that the Sun is farthest north or south of the equator [13]

**\*source** (sôrs) place from which something comes [4]

**species** (spē′shēz) a class of beings that are related because they have similar characteristics [14]

**stars** (stärz) celestial bodies that appear as bright points of light in the night sky [3]

**suction** (suk′shən) a force that sucks a substance (solid, liquid, or gas) into a space [12]

**\*sufficient** (sə fish′ənt) enough to meet a need [18]

**surgery** (sur′jər ē) removal or repair of a part of the body [5]

## T

**temperate** (tem′pər it) maintaining a mild temperature [2]

**theory** (thē′rē) an unproved explanation based on known facts [8]

**tilted** (tilt′əd) leaning at an angle [13]

**tracheophytes** (trā′kē ō fīts′) nonflowering plants that have spores instead of seeds [18]

**transfer** (trans′fur) to move from one person, place, or thing to another [1]

**tropical** (trop′i kəl) found in or typical of a place that has consistently warm weather [2]

**tumors** (tōō′mərz) growths in the body that form when the number of normal body cells increases too quickly [5]

## U

**urine** (yōōr′in ) a clear yellow liquid waste released by the body [17]

---

\* Academic English word

Lesson numbers appear in brackets.

## V

*vary (var′ē) to have different kinds or types [10]

vertically (vur′ti kəl ē) upright; the opposite of *horizontally* [10]

veterinarian (vet′ər ə nār′ē en) a doctor who is trained to care for animals [5]

vitamins (vī′tə minz) natural substances in food that are necessary to keep the body healthy [11]

volcanoes (vol kā′nōz) holes in Earth's surface through which lava, gases, and rock erupt [6]

---

* Academic English word

Lesson numbers appear in brackets.